SALFORD'S
TRAMWAYS
-- PART ONE --

A history of local road passenger transport in and around Salford from the days of the horse drawn omnibus to the development of electric tramway system 1824 - 1912

EDWARD GRAY

Copyright © 1997 Foxline Publishing and Edward Gray
ISBN 1 870119 47 9
All rights reserved
Designed by G. K.Fox
Typeset by Bill Rear
Printed by the Amadeus Press, Huddersfield

Published by Foxline Publishing
32 Urwick Road, Romiley, Stockport. SK6 3JS

SALFORD'S TRAMWAYS

Contents

<<< Salford's first electric tramcars were supplied In 1901-02 by the Birkenhead firm of G.F. Milnes. Car number 79 is seen here in original condition at the Frederick Road Depot entrance. The cars were finished in maroon (chocolate) and cream, with panels lined out in gold and blue. The clip-on enamel route indicator may be noted on the end of the top deck, below the wrought-ironwork surround.

1
Turnpike Roads and
Early Omnibus Schemes

The origins of the local public transport system may be traced to the road improvement schemes of the latter half of the eighteenth century and to the enterprise of the Greenwood family of Pendleton.

The growth of towns and the increase of trade in the region had led to large-scale projects to improve communications in the 1700s. Travel by road was arduous and slow, so projects to make the rivers Mersey and Irwell navigable from the tidal estuary near Warrington had been proposed. The Mersey & Irwell Navigation scheme to deepen the rivers as far as the Old Quay area of Salford (between Blackfriars and Irwell Street) gained approval in 1721. Work began in 1724, but progress was slow because of the shallow and winding nature of the rivers, and the need to construct locks and weirs at several points. Nevertheless, by 1734 small sea-going vessels were able to use some 22 miles of the river system between Salford and the entrance lock on the Mersey estuary, and the carriage of goods by water was thus facilitated. By 1759 work had begun on the Duke of Bridgewater's canal project, the original intention of which was to follow a route from Worsley which would have remained north of the river, to terminate on land between Irwell Street and Ordsall Lane. From there it could have been connected to the river navigation by means of a lock. (Construction was, in fact, begun with this intention, but a change of plan altered the course of the canal from Monton onwards to take it over the Mersey & Irwell Navigation at Barton, thence to Stretford to turn northwards and terminate at Castlefield on the Manchester side of the river. A connection to the river navigation was made at Cornbrook, and later at Hulme.) By 1776 the Duke had constructed an extension of his canal to the Mersey estuary at Runcorn, thus breaking the monopoly of the river navigation, and providing an alternative route which had the advantages of a constant depth of water, freedom from shallows and assorted obstructions, and which, by following the contours of the land, did not need any locks except at the Runcorn terminus.

The continued growth of industry, and the consequent increase in the transport of raw materials and manufactured goods, made it necessary to find some method of improving land-based communications also. Obligations on each parish for the upkeep of the roads in its area were frequently avoided, and the highways were little more than cart tracks. Goods were moved by pack horses, carts being used only for short distances, as their wheels created difficulties over soft surfaces, and the roads were often impassable after wet weather. Those few people who did travel made their way on foot or by horseback.

The Pendleton Turnpike Trust, 1753

'Turnpiking' of roads was already common in the south of England by 1725. This was a solution to the problem of keeping the roads in passable condition, whereby payment was exacted from road users in return for keeping the road surfaces in good repair. The 'turnpikes' were gates set across the road at intervals to halt the progress of those liable to pay tolls, but before anyone could erect such barriers, individual Acts of Parliament were required. On the 31st October 1752 there was a meeting of local businessmen to plan an application to Parliament for permission to turnpike roads in the Salford area. This was duly passed in 1753 and gave powers to improve the main highways spreading fan-wise from Salford to Warrington (along what is now Eccles Old Road, through Eccles and Irlam); to Wigan and Chorley (via Irlams O'Th'Height and Swinton); from Swinton as far as Broadoak on the Worsley Road (the old way to Wigan, though the portion on to Worsley and Astley was not included at this date); and to Bolton (via Pendlebury). The company formed to improve these roads took the title of The Pendleton Turnpike Trust. At first, their sole toll bar was opposite Pendleton Pole, near the present St.Thomas's Church, but even this led to numerous objections from local landowners and farmers, though it would seem likely that road users would have been able to take advantage of several miles of improved roads in the district without paying a toll at all unless they passed through Pendleton.

In the following year, 1754, on the other side of the Irwell Valley, the road to Bury (now Bury Old Road) was the subject of a similar Turnpike Act, but it was another thirty years before a 1784 Act approved the road over Agecroft Bridge to link the roads from Rochdale to Warrington, enabling through traffic to avoid Manchester. The 1784 Act also permitted the erection of additional toll bars on the roads covered by the 1753 Act. The bar at Pendleton was moved to the junction of the Eccles and the Bolton roads, where gates were constructed across each road separately, perhaps an indication of the amount of traffic at busy times.

The Manchester Bolton & Bury Canal

Carriage by water remained attractive, particularly for bulk commodities, and the increase in demand for coal following the introduction of steam engines in the mills in the 1790s, led to the construction of a canal to link Salford, Bolton and Bury with the collieries of the Irwell Valley. There was no road along the valley bottom at the time, for the turnpike roads ran along the crests at each side, just as the main roads do today, but there had long been mining in the Clifton district, and it was known that there were considerable reserves of coal at other points in the valley. In order to provide an outlet for this coal, and with the intention of making a junction with the Mersey & Irwell Navigation, an Act of 1791 authorised the construction of the Manchester, Bolton and Bury Canal. The section between Oldfield Road and Clifton, via Windsor Bridge, Pendleton and Agecroft, was in use by 1795, and packet boat services for passengers between Salford and Bolton began over the full length in the following year. The main traffic, as forecast, was from the mines at Clifton, Kearsley, Agecroft and Pendleton, some of the pits being so close to the canal bank that coal could be transferred direct from the pit-head into canal barges. The projected link with the Irwell was accomplished in 1808 by a series of six locks sited between the river (near the present Prince's Bridge) and the terminal wharves at Oldfield Road.

Irwell Bridges

Bridges over the Irwell connecting Salford with Manchester were also being augmented and improved. Originally, there was only the narrow Salford Bridge, built of wood in 1365, and later replaced by a stone structure of 1538, which was widened in 1776. This was in its turn replaced by the present Victoria Bridge in 1839. The first New Bailey Street Bridge had been allowed by Act of Parliament in 1765, and carried a toll until 1803 - this was replaced by the present Albert Bridge in 1844. Regent Bridge opened in 1808 and carried a toll until 1855. Waterloo Bridge, linking Greengate with Strangeways, had at first been a cast-iron structure, carrying a toll until 1865, when it was purchased and rebuilt by the Corporations of Salford and Manchester. The original Blackfriars foot-bridge of 1761 was replaced in 1819-20 and freed from toll in 1848. Broughton Bridge of 1806 carried a toll until 1872. Other bridges over the Irwell at Cromwell Road, Wallness Road (Frederick Road), Chapel Street (Palatine Bridge), Irwell Street, Hampson Street (Prince's Bridge), and Trafford Road, were all built by the municipal authorities in the latter part of the nineteenth century, and were never subject to tolls.

Turnpike Road Construction And Tolls

By 1784 the Pendleton Trust was responsible for over 23 miles of highway in the area. The methods adopted by the Trust to improve the roads varied. The 'pavement' type of construction advocated by Telford consisted of stone blocks laid end-to-end, sometimes with shallow channels incorporated to guide the wheels. McAdam's system was to lay a covering of broken rock or gravel, which was cheaper than the stone blocks, but which was not as suitable for heavy loads. The Pendleton Trust used both methods, sometimes in conjunction, as, for example, in the Irlams O'Th'Height and Swinton districts, where there were stretches with stone pavements each

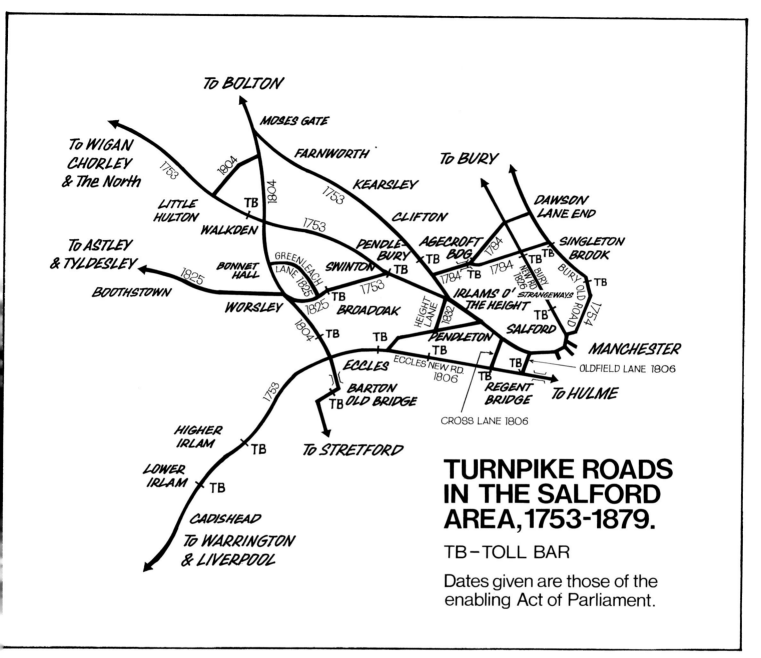

TURNPIKE ROADS IN THE SALFORD AREA, 1753-1879.

TB – TOLL BAR

Dates given are those of the enabling Act of Parliament.

Map of the Turnpike Roads in the Salford Area (1753 - 1879) *A. Palmer.*

three yards wide at the sides of the road, with a four-yard-wide central section of gravel.

At first, tolls were collected by the gate-keepers on behalf of the Trust. The scale of fees was normally displayed on a board fixed to the wall of the toll-keeper's house. Travellers on foot were allowed through free of charge except at bridges, where sometimes only local residents were accorded this privilege), but other tolls levied could range from two shillings and eight pence for a waggon with wheels less than six inches wide, to one shilling for a similar waggon with wider wheels (the wide wheels did less damage to the roads) ; from one shilling and sixpence for a coach drawn by six horses, to four pence for a coach drawn by only one horse ; from ten pence per score for cattle, to five pence per score for sheep, to one penny per horse without a cart. At a later stage, the privilege of collecting the tolls was sometimes put out to tender, and the Trust's income would then be rents received from the lessees, rather than the total receipts from the traffic. As

an example, the right to levy tolls at the gate near Agecroft Bridge was offered for £100 in 1803, and the revenue rose to between two hundred and three hundred pounds per annum by the middle of the century. In contrast, the builders of the first New Bailey Street bridge were able to lease their tolls for a much higher figure (£1,150 during the final year, also 1803), as their bridge occupied a site at the busiest spot along the river, not many yards from the traders of the original Salford Quay, and also the point at which the packet boats for passengers arrived and departed. The highest total income received by the Pendleton Trust for its roads in any one year was £8700, the receipts diminishing as tolls were abolished and powers expired towards the 1870s.

Additional Turnpike Acts

Further Turnpike Acts had followed as the network of roads spread and useful connections or improvements were made. Additions came in 1804 for the Barton - Worsley - Moses Gate road; in 1806 the Eccles New Road to Hulme, via the new Regent Bridge (opened 1808), and including Cross Lane and Oldfield Lane (now Oldfield Road); in 1825 the Broadoak to Worsley and Astley extension, including Greenleach Lane; and in 1826 the Bury New Road.

Stage Coach And Canal Services For Passengers

The improvement in the road surfaces brought about by the establishment of the Turnpike Trusts stimulated the long-distance stage-coach traffic for mail and passengers, but even so the journeys were long and tiresome, and patronised by only a few. The first service in the area is thought to have begun in 1772-3, when a coach left the 'Spread Eagle' Hotel in Salford for Liverpool on Mondays, Wednesdays and Fridays, returning on Tuesdays, Thursdays and Saturdays. Passengers had to present themselves at the inn by 6.00 a.m. They would breakfast at Irlam, dine at Warrington, drink tea at Prescot, and reach Liverpool at nightfall - a long and rough ride. It was not surprising that competition soon appeared in the shape of horse-drawn sail-assisted packet boats on the Mersey & Irwell Navigation, departing at 8.00 a.m. from the New Bailey Street landing stage and arriving in Runcorn eight hours later, from where passengers for Liverpool could travel on across the Mersey by sailing ship. The Duke of Bridgewater also competed for passengers by offering packet services along his canal, as also did the proprietors of the Manchester, Bolton and Bury Canal from 1796. Vessels on this latter canal were described as "elegant passage boats for passengers and their luggage only," and left from New Windsor, Salford, for Bolton at 5.00 p.m. in summer, or 4.00 p.m. winter, taking three hours for the journey at a fare of one-shilling-and-sixpence in the "front room" or one-shilling in the "back room." The flow of passenger traffic may be adduced from the fact that the morning journey was in the opposite direction, from Bolton to Salford, leaving at 6.00 a.m. on market days, 7.00 a.m. on other days.

However, coaches could travel over routes where no water service was possible. By 1781 there was a daily service to Chorley and Blackpool, run by Pickford & Co., which connected at Preston with the coach for Lancaster, Penrith and Carlisle. Further road improvements saw over twenty coaches running daily on the Liverpool route, and new services to Bolton, Blackburn, Bury, Leigh, Wigan and Southport were begun. By the 1820s the journey time to Liverpool had been reduced to four hours and twenty minutes, and the coaches were able to maintain a speed of up to twelve miles per hour on some routes. The fare from Salford to Bolton was six shillings, to Liverpool eighteen shillings. A 'small parcel' could be sent on this latter journey for one shilling.

With the application of steam power to manufactures, an immense impetus was given to the industrial development of the region. To produce economically, it was necessary to concentrate machinery in large urban factories, and the movement of population towards the towns accelerated. In 1801 the combined population of Manchester and Salford totalled nearly 116,000; by 1820, when there were over one hundred spinning mills in the district, this figure had almost doubled. As yet, however, the housing areas had not spread far beyond the city centres, and there was very little demand for local short-distance transport, most people residing within walking distance of their place of work. The highways remained largely free of passenger traffic, but the rise of a new middle class and their migration towards residential districts in the outer suburbs, gradually led to a visible need for some form of short-distance local transport service, as distinct from the long-distance stage coach routes. John Greenwood, of Pendleton, was the first man to cater for this need.

John Greenwood, 1788 - 1851

John Greenwood, born at Wadsworth Moor, near Heptonstall, Yorkshire, in 1788, had originally been apprenticed to a corn miller, but having injured his hand in a shotgun accident, he left that trade to become a toll collector

The original toll-gate at Pendleton was situated opposite St. Thomas's Church, but at a later stage this was dismantled, and two separate bars were erected across the entrances to Bolton Road and Eccles Old Road. This photograph was taken towards the end of the turnpike era about 1870, and shows the gates on Eccles Old Road, looking towards Pendleton Church. The toll collector's house is on the left, with the original Woolpack Inn lying out of the picture beyond. The Bolton Road gates were on the other side of the inn, with a separate collector's house. The 'big lamp' in front of the inn may be seen centre left.

at Burnley, afterwards moving to Pendleton in the same capacity. Later, with Joshua Bower, of Leeds, as his partner, he successfully bid for the lease to collect tolls at the turnpikes at the fork of the Bolton and Eccles roads at Pendleton, and it was whilst engaged in these duties that he became aware of the increasing movement of people from the suburbs towards the business centres of Manchester. Accordingly, on the 1st January 1824 he instituted the first omnibus service, operating a vehicle described as "little more than a box on wheels" between Pendleton and Market Street, Manchester. The vehicle locally was called the "Pow Mail," after its starting point opposite Pendleton Pole ('Pow'), which stood on the site later occupied by St.Thomas's Church.

This novel omnibus service operated several times a day at a fare of sixpence, which, though not cheap for 1824, was good value when compared to the stage-coach charges per mile, and much cheaper than the city hackney coach fares. Greenwood's venture had several innovative features, departing radically from established stage-coach practices, whose operators had to work from fixed stopping points, usually coaching inns, and fill a high proportion of seats to make their service economically viable. As the new service took up and set down passengers at any point along the route, it was easy to use, and there was no delay in boarding or alighting. Intending passengers did not have to make their way to, and wait at, an inn; nor did they need to visit a booking office. The fare could be paid on the spot. Travellers could rely on the speed and punctuality of the service, though the duties of the driver were described as being 'somewhat arduous,' for besides handling his horses, he had to alight from his box to open the door for passengers as they boarded or left the vehicle, announce his progress by blowing a horn at intervals along the route, collect the fares and afterwards account for them at the office. A story was told at the time of a disgruntled coachman who arrived in Greenwood's office to hand in his takings, but thinking 'the boss' was out, began to count his money in the presence of a fellow-driver, dividing the coins into two equal piles, saying, "This is for the boss, this is for me." There was an odd shilling over. Said the coachman, "I'll toss up whether the boss has it or me. Heads for the boss, tails for me." Heads won, but the coachman then said, "That's not fair. I'll toss again." Greenwood had overheard this talk, and immediately rushed in, saying, "No, no, it's mine, and I'll have it." What happened to the coachman was not recorded, but the habit of some drivers of handing in only a portion of the amount collected, always provided a source of conflict. Greenwood was once on record as commenting that, as he had to find all the expenses, he wished his men would let him have 'one wheel in four.'

The 1824 service was an immediate success. The first omnibuses with their limited accommodation, were soon superseded by larger vehicles which could accommodate eight or nine inside, plus three or four with the driver. The fare inside remained at sixpence, but was reduced to fourpence for 'outside' passengers. Greenwood was also encouraged to expand his undertaking by operating on new routes to Eccles, Swinton and Bolton.In co-operation with Henry Clough, William Howarth and Robert Turner, he also inaugurated services on the Broughton and Cheetham Hill routes from Manchester. The opening of the Liverpool & Manchester Railway in 1830 destroyed the long-distance stage coach services between those towns - by 1832 only one stage coach was in regular service to Liverpool, and that was for parcels rather than passengers. The opening of other railway lines had similar effects in other districts, and the turnpike roads suffered a sharp decline in fortune. In contrast, however, omnibuses operating on the short local routes prospered, not least on services to the railway stations. Inevitably, success attracted competitors to the most profitable stretches of road, and by 1836 there were seven other coach owners offering services on the Manchester to Bolton route. In addition to Greenwood's local routes, a Manchester to Worsley service was operated twice daily by J.Brookes, and another to Barton, also twice daily, by W.Phillips.

About 1837 John Greenwood had become the host of the Horse Shoe Tavern, situated at the corner of Church Street, opposite to St.Thomas's Church, Pendleton, which had been consecrated in 1831. Alongside the inn, Greenwood built a waiting room for passengers and a small office, where his sons John and Henry worked. At the tavern, his men 'could have a pint of ale for the paying for,' and it was reported that 'Old John' believed that 'a gill of good ale was worth a whole brewery of water.' Behind the inn was an extensive coach yard and stables, where at night Greenwood kept a solitary cow amongst the horses, grazing it elsewhere during the day. The milk yield from the cow was divided between the inhabitants of the inn and Greenwood's two sisters, who lived nearby. 'Old John,' a stout man of a restless alert nature, was often to be seen at the entrance to his office, distinctively attired in corduroy kneebreeches, white shirt, and coloured stockings, keeping his eye on the traffic. One son, Henry, died young, but

the other son, John, junior, although originally destined for a career in the textile industry, left to join his father's expanding business. By 1849, Greenwood owned no fewer than 177 horses, and was the most important omnibus proprietor in the region. He was also a partner in several leases of turnpike tolls in various parts of Lancashire, Cheshire and Derbyshire, as well as of the bridges at Conway and Bangor in North Wales. In due course, as his obituary put it, 'Old John passed his last gate. With manly resignation he bowed to the Divine Will on the 23rd May 1851,' leaving his son, 'Young John,' at the age of 33 in sole charge of the omnibus undertaking and with partnerships in the toll contracts. The man who was fond of claiming that it was he who had first taught the local people to 'lose the use of their legs' had passed on.

John Greenwood, Junior, 1818 - 1886

John Greenwood, junior, born in Pendleton on the 12th May 1818, inherited the business at a time of increasing rivalry. In 1850 he had married Helen, daughter of Mr.Thomas Walker, corn factor, of Leaf Square, and moved into Heath Cottage at the corner of Broad Street and Brindle Heath Road, opposite his father's tavern, from where he was ideally placed to supervise the business. Unlike his father, he neither drank nor smoked, but he appeared to have inherited his father's business capacity. At this time there were some 64 omnibuses competing for passengers along the main roads into Manchester, but 'Young John' was ready to meet any challenge. He was soon faced with an unexpected threat when in 1852 a competitor arrived from Scotland to set up the City Omnibus Company, using larger three-horse omnibuses with accommodation for 42 (17 inside, 25 on the 'knifeboard' seat on top) and charging a fare of only threepence. These new vehicles were constructed without the rear door, which had previously been considered indispensable, and the outside 'knifeboard' seat, reached by a iron ladder at the rear, was raised, so that no longer did the feet of the top deck passengers have to dangle in front of the side windows.'Young John' immediately set off for Edinburgh to purchase similar roomy vehicles with which to defend his share of the traffic, and soon the routes were fairly peaceably divided between the main competitors. Afterwards, he set up his own coach-building establishment on Ford Lane, close to his residence. Greenwood operated mainly on the Salford, Eccles, Swinton and Pendlebury services, but with one route from Manchester Exchange to Brooks's Bar, whilst Robert Turner, with premises on Bury New Road, had captured the Higher Broughton, Lower Broughton, Cheetham Hill, Prestwich and Whitefield traffic after his temporary partnership with Greenwood had been dissolved.

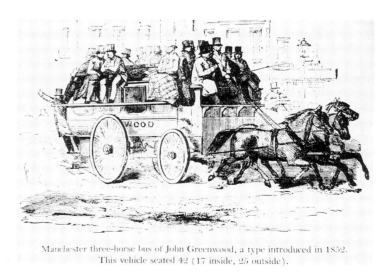

Manchester three-horse bus of John Greenwood, a type introduced in 1852.
This vehicle seated 42 (17 inside, 25 outside).

In 1852 John Greenwood, Junior, introduced a larger type of omnibus, seating 42, 17 inside and 25 outside. The outside passengers were charged a lower fare, but had to reach their precarious longitudonal seat by way of a vertical iron ladder at the rear of the coach. Their feet rested upon a long footboard, and passengers paying the higher fare objected to the view of legs gained from inside the coach.

Fierce competition between the omnibus proprietors surfaced again in 1857 during the period of the Art Treasures Exhibition at Old Trafford, when there was a great demand for public transport to and from the exhibition site. There were complaints of overloading, overcharging, and dangerous racing between coaches. At this time James Standring, a coal merchant, began to operate omnibuses, and when the exhibition closed, he transferred his vehicles to Greenwood's Pendleton and Brooks's Bar routes, and to Turner's route to Cheetham Hill. The rivalry culminated in a series of races between Standring's vehicles and those of Greenwood and Turner, with onlookers cheering on their favourites. The Police initiated a series of prosecutions for dangerous driving, and local magistrates were also determined to stamp out instances of street betting on the omnibus races. Standring prospered well enough to be able to give up his coal business and concentrate on his omnibus services, which eventually settled on routes from Manchester Exchange to All Saints and Old Trafford.

It was in this period that John Greenwood, junior, was responsible for another innovation. The Pendleton Post Office closed at 8.15 p.m. and, as this was thought to be too early for users of the postal service, a 'free letter bag' was attached to the last omnibus of the day, 9.30 p.m. from Pendleton. Persons wishing to post letters could place them in the bag on the rear of the omnibus at it passed along the route. On reaching Market Street, Manchester, the bag was removed and taken to the sorting department of the main post office in Brown Street, where letters were dealt with in time to be on board the London Mail train that same night. No charge was made for this service.

Greenwood continued to adopt an enterprising policy, sending coaches to London to share in the profitable traffic during the time of the second Great Exhibition, and later co-operating with the company building the railway from Manchester to Chester, running omnibuses in conjunction with the trains from the rail-head, wherever that happened to have reached, to the Chester terminus until the line was complete.

He and Turner continued to share a 'Central Office' at 31, Market Street, Manchester, at which point their routes from the suburbs terminated. Advertisements of the period indicate that both businesses claimed to have been established since 1824, and that both were able to supply 'elegant equipages,' horses with 'richly chased silver harness,' and drivers and footmen 'in and out of livery' for weddings, funerals, picnics, and any form of cab or carriage private hire work. Turner's advertisements listed branch establishments at Shude Hill, Higher Broughton, Whitefield, Middleton, and Harpurhey, with a Head Office and Works at Cheetham Hill. Greenwood's Head Office and Works remained at Pendleton, with branch offices at Windsor Bridge, Salford ; College Land, St.Mary's, Manchester ; and at 256 Stretford New Road.

An advertisement from an 1858 Directory shows the extent of Greenwood's business interests and the range of services offered. The 'Central Office' at 31 Market Street was shared with Robert Turner, who operated similar services in the Broughton area from his establishment on Bury New Road.

ESTABLISHED 1824.
MANCHESTER & SALFORD OMNIBUS & POST HORSE ESTABLISHMENT.
JOHN GREENWOOD

Begs respectfully to inform the Gentry and Inhabitants of Manchester and the Public generally, that he keeps for Hire every description of Carriage, both for private and public service.

WEDDINGS supplied with ELEGANT EQUIPAGES, and FIRST-CLASS HORSES, with Richly Chased SILVER HARNESS.

DRIVERS AND FOOTMEN IN AND OUT OF LIVERY.

FUNERALS FURNISHED WITH NEAT HEARSES AND MOURNING CARRIAGES,
BLACK HORSES FOR MUTES, &C.

J. G., in order to execute this branch of his business in a respectable style, has procured on the Continent a number of valuable Black Horses, well adapted for this description of work.

PRIVATE CARRIAGES AND CARRIAGE HORSES LET BY THE MONTH OR YEAR.

Professional Gentlemen Contracted with for Cab or Carriage Work.—Pic-Nic Parties supplied with Private Omnibuses.
POST HORSES ALWAYS IN READINESS.

Orders received at the Central Office, 31, Market Street ; the Branch Establishments, 256, Stretford New Road ; College Land, St. Mary's, MANCHESTER ; and at Windsor Bridge, SALFORD. Head Office and Works, PENDLETON.

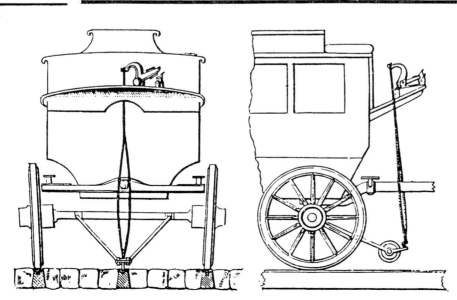

NEW STREET RAILWAY AT MANCHESTER, WITH OMNIBUS PERAMBULATOR.

Diagram of Haworth's Patent Perambulating System reproduced in the "Illustrated London News" of the 16th November 1861.

Although the efforts of the Turnpike Trusts had considerably improved the road surfaces, the cobble stones or setts still gave a rough and very noisy ride. The railways had already demonstrated the advantages of the smooth rail, and John Greenwood, Junior, and his brother-in-law, John Haworth, began to investigate the possibilities of placing metal rails into existing roadways. The main difficulty was in finding a method of keeping the wheels of the omnibus on the rail and off the stones.

In Birkenhead in August 1860 George Francis Train, an American, had attempted to solve the same problem by laying a street tramway using L-shaped rails. The upright portion of Train's step-rail was successful in guiding the carriage wheels along the horizontal portion, but the space between the rails was at a lower level than the rest of the road surface, thereby causing difficulties for the passage of other street traffic. Greenwood and Haworth sought to minimise this difficulty by laying rails, or plateways, flush with the road surface, but with a third centre rail, grooved to accommodate a small guide wheel fixed beneath the omnibuses. The guide wheel was designed to drop into the groove and so keep the four outer wheels running along the smooth surface of the plates. Thus, there would be no need for flanges on either the rails or the wheels, and there would be nothing to obstruct the passage of other vehicles. The scheme was registered as "Haworth's Patent Perambulating System." Greenwood applied to the Pendleton Turnpike Trustees for permission to construct a double line of such a tramway from his Pendleton office along Broad Street to a point near Cross Lane at the boundary of the Salford and Pendleton townships, and to the Salford Town Council for permission to continue the double line over Windsor Bridge, along The Crescent and Chapel Street, to Albert Bridge in New Bailey Street.

A specimen portion of track, one hundred yards long, was laid in Broad Street for the inspection of the authorities. An omnibus was driven over the track, and it was demonstrated how the 'perambulator,' or guide wheel could be fitted to the leading axle of existing vehicles. The driver was enabled to raise or lower the guide wheel by means of a rod or chain passing through the footboard whenever he wished to leave or join the rails. The Salford District Surveyor, accompanied by members of the Highways sub-committee, also journeyed to Birkenhead to inspect the street railway there and to compare the two systems. In the subsequent public discussion on the rival merits of the two schemes, another disadvantage of the Birkenhead street railway became apparent. In an issue of the 'Salford Weekly News' in December 1860, a correspondent, in commending Haworth's proposals, cited an article in 'The Engineer' and said, "It appears that while you are constructing a railway on Mr. Train's plan, you are also making a canal," a sarcastic reference to the pools of water which collected in the sunken portion of roadway between the step rails. After rain, the writer noted, "the 'canal,' shallow at first, deepens with the constant tread of horses' feet, and at length becomes navigable." It was the consensus of opinion that a tramway on Haworth's principle would be an advantage for the omnibus traffic. Accordingly, it was recommended to the full Borough Council in March 1861 that permission should be given to Mr. John Greenwood to lay down his tramway, subject to certain conditions about the maintenance of the road surface and access to drains, gas and water pipes. The Corporation was to be indemnified against any costs incurred by the work. The sub-committee reached no conclusion about the advisability, or otherwise, of a double-line tramway, however, leaving this for the full Council to decide. The Council, although agreed that "Mr. Haworth's tramway was the most

Illustrations of the 1861 tramway are rare, but this painting in the Salford City Art Gallery, dating from about 1870 shows a Greenwood omnibus as adapted to run on Haworth's Patent Perambulating Principle. The guide wheel may be noted running in the centre groove. The omnibus is depicted passing the Victoria Arch entrance to Peel Park, now the site of the Salford University buildings. This early tramway remained in use until 1872, but being only a single line, when omnibuses proceeding in opposite directions met, one had to leave the rails. (Courtesy City of Salford Museums & Art Gallery.)

feasible of all the street railways that had been projected," erred on the side of caution, and gave permission for only a single line.

The formal agreement was drawn up in June 1861, and stipulated that Greenwood and Haworth would be responsible for the maintenance of the roadway between the rails and for twelve inches either side, a principle which led to a great saving on the rates, and which was continued in later tramway days. The local newspaper of September 1861 reported that, "The line through Pendleton and along The Crescent has been laid for some time, and the smooth easy running afforded to those 'busses running on it has given general satisfaction." Construction of the line along Chapel Street was reported to be proceeding "with vigour," and the whole project was expected to be complete in a few weeks' time.

Unhappily, the fact that the omnibuses had to leave the smooth rails and return to the uneven setts for parts of the journey, or when passing vehicles using the single-line tramway in the opposite direction, mitigated against its complete success, but it nevertheless remained in use until 1872. It is evident from press references that the use of the tramway was not limited to omnibuses on the Pendleton route only, and an accident report indicates, for example, that the Eccles omnibus made use of the rails where available for part of its journey. Haworth, indeed, advocated several schemes for its improvement and renewal, and in 1865 asked for the removal of the 'blue setts' with which the tramway was paved and their substitution by 'grit setts,' which, he said, did not cause the horses to slip. This work was carried out by the Council and charged to the operators, as per the original agreement, with an allowance for those setts taken up which could be used again elsewhere. Later, Haworth produced plans for an improved "Ratepayers' Tramway," which dispensed with the guide wheel principle, thus making it "practical for all to use," he said, and which he wanted to lay down on Regent Road from Cross Lane to St.George's Church, Hulme. The Council resolved to meet the representatives of the Manchester Highways Committee "to ascertain their intentions in the matter."

Formation Of The Manchester Carriage Company 1865

The City Omnibus Company had meantime been purchased by the Manchester alderman Ivie Mackie, who already had a financial interest in Greenwood's business, and it was perhaps inevitable that, in order to eliminate wasteful competition, negotiations for a merger of the interests of Greenwood, Mackie, and Robert and James Turner should result in the formation of a larger company. By this date, Greenwood's stock of horses had increased from 177 in 1849 to over 500 at the time the new Company was formed. Greenwood had prospered sufficiently to enable him to move to grander accommodation at Little Bolton Lodge, Eccles New Road, where he resided with his wife, son (also John), four daughters, one sister-in-law, and two servants. Brother-in-law John Haworth lived nearby, at Mode Wheel House, which, like Little Bolton Lodge, was between Weaste and

Ladywell, on the River Irwell side of Eccles New Road. Greenwood contributed 33 omnibuses to the new joint venture, Mackie 29, and the Turners 29. The title chosen was 'The Manchester Carriage Company,' formed on the 1st March 1865, with Mackie as its first Chairman and John Greenwood, Junior, as Vice-Chairman and Managing Director. John Haworth also became a director. (James Standring's business was absorbed at a later date, after 1869.)

The general offices of the new Company were at Greenwood's premises at 31 Market Street, Manchester. Although at first, the services provided were much the same as had been offered by the individual undertakings, the Company soon reorganised them into 'city' and 'country' routes. In 1866 'city' routes passing through Salford were :-

Higher Broughton, from Market Street, via Bury New Road.
Lower Broughton, from Market Street.
Weaste, from Newton Heath, via Deansgate, Hulme, Regent Road, and Eccles New Road.
Weaste, from Market Street, via Oldfield Road, or Cross Lane.
Pendleton, from Market Street, via Peel Park.

These shorter 'city' routes all had fares of threepence inside and twopence out, there being no fare stages. Passengers were charged the same flat fare for the whole or only part of the journey.

The 'country' routes were those operating over a longer distance. Those passing through Salford and Broughton were :-

Bury, from the Old Boar's Head, Hanging Ditch (fares 9d and 6d).
Bolton, from Market Street, via Pendlebury and Clifton
    (fares : first class 1s; second class 10d; third class 8d.)
Patricroft, from Market Street, via Pendleton and Eccles Old Road
    (fares 4d and 3d.)
Prestwich (Polefield), from Market Street (fares 5d and 3d.)
Radcliffe, from the Old Boar's Head, via Prestwich. (This appears to have been a Sunday-evenings only service.)
Swinton, from Market Street, via Pendleton (fares 6d and 4d.)
Whitefield, from the Old Board's Head, via Prestwich
    (fares : to Whitefield 7d and 5d ; to Prestwich 5d and 3d.)

The 1861 'street railway' remained in use by Company vehicles, but new schemes put forward by Haworth for the improvement or extension of the tramway were not approved. A number of complaints about loose rails had been received by the authorities, and some objectors wanted the tramway to be taken up altogether, but the Council resolved that it was "not desirable to remove the Street Tramway." Greenwood and Haworth had previously suggested that the Salford Highways Committee itself should seek powers to construct further tramways, but no action was taken on this proposal. In November 1869, however, the Carriage Company announced that it intended

In 1865 Greenwood and the other local omnibus proprietors merged their interests to avoid wasteful competition. The Manchester Carriage Company was formed. A comparison with the previous illustration will reveal that this is a former Greenwood omnibus, now displaying the new Company title. It will be noted on these vehicles that the old vertical ladder has been replaced with a curved staircase to enable outside passengers to reach a higher top deck, which removed the necessity for those on the 'knifeboard' seat to dangle their legs in front of the windows. The location is by the Victoria Arch at Peel Park

to apply for Parliamentary powers to lay down tramways on main roads in the area. The Company had in mind a scheme on Haworth's on-and-off principle to allow for the flexible use of their omnibuses, but were prepared to consider an alternative plan using carriages with flanged wheels which would be unable to leave the tracks. Five possible routes which would pass through Salford were proposed :-

1. From Manchester via Regent Bridge - Regent Road - Eccles New Road - Eccles - Liverpool Road - to Patricroft Bridge.
2. From Manchester via Albert Bridge - New Bailey Street - Chapel Street - The Crescent - Pendleton - Eccles Old Road - to join with the above line at Eccles Market Place.
3. Making a junction with the above line at Pendleton - Bolton Road - Irlams O'Th'Height - Manchester Road - Swinton - to Walkden.
4. From Market Street via Victoria Street and Great Ducie Street to Bury New Road and Kersal.
5. Connecting with the above line on Bury New Road (near Waterloo Road) via Broughton Lane, Camp Street, and Lower Broughton Road, to The Cliff.

Companies from London and Liverpool were also said to be interested in promoting similar schemes, but the Borough Council was resistant to the idea, because a major Tramways Bill, which envisaged local authorities constructing and owning their own tramways, was already under discussion in Parliament. The Mayor of Salford, in response to a number of complaints about the lack of repairs on the 1861 tramway, replied that *"It is not likely that the Company will do much during the time of suspense concerning the Tramway."*

In November 1869, the Pendleton Turnpike Trust applied to Parliament for permission to make certain branch turnpike roads, and asked for powers to retain the toll bars. The gates at Pendleton on Bolton Road and Eccles Old Road were said to have receipts upwards of £2500 per annum. A correspondent writing in the 'Salford Weekly News' supported the application for the continuance of the Trust's powers, and suggested that the advantages of living in Pendleton should be extended to Salford beyond the boundary near Cross Lane. In the Trust's area, he claimed, the roads were swept at least once a month, maintained in good condition, and in summer watered to keep down the dust. In the event, the Trust's powers were continued for one year only.

In December 1869 John Greenwood, Junior, succeeded to the Chairmanship of the Company, and pressed the Council to reconstruct the tramway. A debate in January 1870 included a proposition calling upon the owners to take up the tramway, but this was defeated, and Company and Council agreed to improvement work being put in hand. Unfortunately, because the clauses of the new Tramway Bill were also under discussion about the same time, work on putting the tramway in good working order ceased whilst Council members reconsidered their position. During one debate the Council appeared to have decided that further street tramways would not be of great local advantage. This prompted a strongly-worded editorial in a local newspaper, which compared the "smooth, easy gliding movement" of tramway travel with the jolts and rattles of the omnibus. In reference to Haworth's tramway, it said, "Much maligned as that imperfectly carried-out experiment has been at times, there is no doubt that it affords the most luxurious two miles of public street travelling in the district. Trams on this plan, allowing perambulating vehicles to move readily on and off the line, would have a decided advantage over others, if the rails were more solidly formed." Indeed, it was clear that the 1861 tramway remained in regular use. It was said that on the Pendleton to Market Street route alone, there were omnibuses every 7½ minutes from 8.30 a.m. to 8.30 p.m., with 16 other journeys up to 10.30 p.m., and, with early services, a grand total of some 208 journeys per day. But it was also noted that the provision of only a single track made the omnibuses 'go down the wrong side of the road' on the return journey into Manchester. In February 1870 the Highways Committee agreed to carry out repairs on the dangerous parts of the road surface, but would not incur further expense, because "It is probable that the existing Street Tramway will be removed in a very short time." On the 23rd February 1870, the Salford Borough Council held a special meeting to discuss street tramways, and, as a result, at the end of that month Greenwood was ordered to take up the rails of the Haworth tramway.

Municipal Tramway Schemes 1875

The 1870 Tramways Act duly became law at about the time the powers of the Turnpike Trusts were expiring. The new Act made provision for the general supervision of tramway undertakings by the Board of Trade and for their authorisation by Provisional Orders, which had to be confirmed subsequently by Act of Parliament. By the 1870 Act, the promoters of

A well-laden omnibus on the route from Patricroft to Manchester stands outside the Old Bull's Head Hotel in Church Street, Eccles, about 1872. One can imagine the difficulty experienced by passengers trying to reach the staircase to alight when the vehicle was crowded. Curtains were fitted to protect inside passengers from the rays of the sun. (Courtesy Salford Cultural Services Department.)

tramways were enabled to submit their proposals without the costly procedure of having individual clauses formulated, debated, and modified. It empowered local authorities to construct and own, but not to operate tramways. The lines had to be leased, but there was provision for the compulsory purchase of the undertaking after 21 years, at the then value of the tramway and works, but without any allowance for the possible loss of profits by the lessees. (This provision later held back progress towards the end of the century, when operators felt it no longer worth while to make improvements with compulsory purchase threatened at scrap prices.) Another clause allowed local authorities to exercise the power of veto on any proposal for tramway construction of which they did not approve, with no right of appeal by the proposer. As Greenwood and Haworth had found in their local agreement, tramway undertakings were saddled with the responsibility for the repair of the roadway between the rails and for 18 inches either side, because it was held that the tram horses would wear out the road surface. Consequently, tramway companies had to maintain vast areas of the street surface for the benefit of other road users, as well as themselves.

The use of a rail laid flush with the roadway, which at the same time contained a groove of such small dimensions as to cause no obstruction to other traffic, did much to popularise the idea of tramways. Such a system did not need Haworth's centre guide rail, but it did require special vehicles with a flanged wheel, which could be used only on the tramway. Haworth's 'on-and-off' system, though allowing more flexible use of the omnibuses, was clearly going to be superseded. The Carriage Company began to consider new proposals for the construction of tramways in districts where the local authorities were not eager to build their own lines, and sub-committees of the Salford and Manchester Town Councils met to consider the possibilities of tramway lines connecting the two towns.

In the meantime, Greenwood had been threatened with a lawsuit because of his failure to take up the 1861 tramway and make good the road surface. The Borough Surveyor was instructed to use Corporation workmen to remove the rails and re-pave the roadways concerned, such work to be at the expense of the Carriage Company. By the end of April 1872 the tramway had been removed and a pioneering venture was over. In July 1872 John Haworth attended a meeting of the Salford Town Council and asked that the Carriage Company should be relieved of the cost of making good the roadway. The request was refused.

The deliberations of the two Town Councils resulted in Acts of 1875, giving powers to construct a joint tramway from Pendleton to the Manchester boundary at Albert Bridge, New Bailey Street (along the line of John Greenwood's original 1824 omnibus route, and of his son's 1861 tramway) and on via Bridge Street, Deansgate, Great Ducie Street, and Bury New Road, to Higher Broughton, making a continuous line from Pendleton to Kersal Bar. It was agreed that work on this line should commence first, although the 1875 Salford Tramways and Improvements Act also included

powers for lines to Irlams O'Th'Height via Bolton Road ; to Eccles from Pendleton via Eccles Old Road ; to Eccles via Regent Road and Eccles New Road ; to Broughton Spout (a point north of Cromwell Bridge, near The Priory at the Cliff) via Lower Broughton Road ; and in Cross Lane and Oldfield Road. The lines were to be leased at an annual rental of 10% of the cost of construction, and there was provision for the lessees to take on the same terms any other lines which the Corporation saw fit to construct.

The Salford Town Clerk and the Borough Surveyor were instructed to obtain information from other towns about the working and leasing of tramways, and details were supplied by Bristol and Birmingham. In February 1876 council members visited the Leeds tramways, and decided to adopt the same method of track construction. The estimated cost was £2500 per mile of single track in paved streets, rising to £5000 per mile in unpaved areas, and it was thought that it would take about six months to complete the two Salford sections of the first chosen route, Pendleton to Albert Bridge and Kersal Bar to the Manchester boundary at the Grove Inn on Bury New Road, whilst the Manchester authority would work on the central portion within that city limits. The two authorities agreed that the title should be 'The Manchester & Salford Tramways.' The fares were not to exceed 3d inside or 2d outside, and, as required by Act of Parliament, the lessees would run at least two carriages each way every morning and evening not later than 7.00 a.m. nor earlier than 6.00 p.m. "for the use of the labouring classes."

The Manchester Carriage Company, already operating omnibus services along the chosen roads, was the obvious candidate to work the new tramway, but a serious disagreement had arisen. When the Corporation plans were made known, the Company had argued that only the Pendleton to Deansgate section should be constructed, and that this should be considered as an experiment. The Company felt that lighter traffic on the Higher Broughton route did not offer the same prospect for revenue, and that the single track with passing loops, as planned for Bury New Road, would lead to delays. It was argued that with only a single track the new tramcars would be able to run only at the frequency of the existing omnibus service, and takings would not increase. On the contrary, profit would diminish if rental for the lines had to be deducted from income. Therefore the Company wished to operate only on the Pendleton line. It was not alone in holding this view, for the Glasgow Tramways Company also made an enquiry, and it, too, was interested only in the Pendleton route. However, the two Corporations would not agree to any alteration of the plans, nor would they consider separate operators for each section of the route. The Company also had reservations about having to take on lease any further lines the Corporation chose to construct, and felt, reasonably, that it should have a voice in any future plans.

In the event, on the 17th August 1876 the two Corporations jointly agreed to award the lease to Mr.Daniel Busby and Mr.William Turton. At this date the lines had not been constructed, and the lease was to run for 21 years from

The Manchester Carriage Company experimented with some longer routes. This vehicle is travelling from Pendleton to Ashton, via Manchester. Notice the stove-pipe hats of the gentlemen, and the conductor with cash bag and uniform cap.

the 31st May 1877. Busby and Turton were already well-known in the tramway world. Busby was an important carriage proprietor from Liverpool, and Turton had a similar business in Leeds. Together they had become enthusiastic tramway promoters in several British towns. Having gained the lease, Busby and Turton promptly urged the construction of other lines. The Manchester Council decided that no further tramways would be considered until there had been experience of working the first line, and until they had a binding contract with someone to work all the routes. The Salford Council, on the other hand, resolved to proceed with a line from Regent Bridge to the Eccles boundary in Eccles New Road near Ladywell, and urged the Barton & Eccles Local Board to continue this line into their district as far as Patricroft. A line planned along Oldfield Road between Chapel Street and Regent Road, would connect this new route with the first line. 'The Manchester Suburban Tramways Company,' (formed by Busby, Turton, John Greenwood, Benjamin Whitworth, M.P., etc.) set about applying for powers to construct tramways outside the Manchester boundary, with the hope of making connection with future Corporation lines to the city centre.

Construction Of The First Lines

In December 1876 Salford accepted the tender of W.J.Thompson of Sheffield to construct the first line at a cost of £9627, the Corporation presumably accepting responsibility for the paving work. The method of construction chosen was that patented by Joseph Kincaid, by which the rails were fixed to a series of chairs sunk into the roadway at intervals of three feet and embedded in concrete. The rails were three-and-a-half inches wide, with a tread or rolling surface of one-and-three-quarter inches, a groove of one-and-a-quarter inches, and an inner edge of half-an-inch. This inner edge had a corrugated surface, the 'wavy guard,' to prevent the horses from slipping. The rails were drilled and fastened to the chairs with wrought-iron spikes. The standard gauge of 4 feet 8½ inches was chosen, and where a double line was built, there was a space of four feet between the two tracks.

Early in January 1877 Busby and Turton exhibited a specimen tramway car at the Fire/Police Station in Chapel Street. It weighed two tons, and offered seating accommodation for 40 passengers, 20 inside and 20 on top. It was duly inspected by Council officials and deemed satisfactory. It had been built by the Starbuck Company of Birkenhead. The founder of this Company, George Starbuck had been connected with G.F.Train's Birkenhead tramway. He was, like Train, an American, and the first tramcars had been imported from the United States. Starbuck set up his own works in the town, said to be the first 'tramcar manufactory' outside the United States, and was able to take advantage of the boom years of the horse tramway construction.

He was now instructed to proceed with the rest of the order for the 30 cars needed for the opening of the Pendleton to Higher Broughton route. Work on the construction of the tramway proceeded, but Busby and Turton did not appear to make any effort to acquire stables or depot premises - instead they entered into secret negotiations with the Carriage Company, and in April 1877, when the opening of the first line was imminent, they agreed to sell to the Company all their concessions and interests in tramways in Manchester, Salford and surrounding districts. This did not please the two Councils, whose members believed that the lessees had no right to sub-let or re-lease their rights to other parties without the consent of the Corporations. But, for the moment, the authorities were powerless to take action if they wanted their new tramway to open on time. The only official intimation which had been made concerning the new arrangement, was that the Carriage Company had agreed to provide the horses, but rumours were rife, and it was clear that Company employees and premises were also to be used.

The Opening Of The First Municipal Tramway

Major-General C.S.Hutchinson, appointed by the Board of Trade, arrived on Tuesday, the 15th May 1877 to inspect as much of the tramway as had been completed. He was able to board a tramcar at The Woolpack Inn, Pendleton, and travel via Manchester as far as the Grove Inn, the line further along Bury New Road to Kersal being as yet unfinished. At 4.30 p.m. on the following Thursday, the 17th May, the members of the two Tramways Committees met at Pendleton Town Hall before boarding the first three of the thirteen tramcars then delivered, to travel to the Grove Inn and formally declare the line open. The local newspaper recorded the fact that the remaining ten tramcars "were taken possession of indiscriminately by such of the spectators as happened to be lucky enough to secure seats." At the Grove Inn, the horses were harnessed to the opposite ends of the cars, and the civic party returned to Deansgate and a celebratory meal in the then new Manchester Town Hall.

Public services began the following day, Friday the 18th May. It was announced that the route, when completed, was to be worked in two separate sections, and that 15 tramcars would work the Deansgate to Pendleton portion, and a similar number the Higher Broughton service, though it was promised that two workmen's cars would run early morning and evening right through from Broughton to Pendleton. The new cars were said to be very handsome and well-patronised. Busby and Turton requested approval for additional short lengths of track so that the tramcars could pass into the premises of the Carriage Company in Church Street, Pendleton, and in Knoll Street, Higher Broughton. These were sites formerly occupied by Greenwood and Turner respectively, and were now to be used to each house 15 tramcars for the two portions of the route, in addition to the Company omnibuses and horses already stabled there. Major-General Hutchinson returned to inspect and approve the Grove Inn to Kersal section of the line on the 3rd July, but the service on this length did not, in fact, begin until Monday the 30th July, and then with only eight tramcars, delivery of the remaining vehicles having been delayed.

As soon as the Higher Broughton section opened, however, it was clear that the reservations expressed by the Carriage Company had been correct. The single track with passing loops along Bury New Road proved unsatisfactory. The intended five-minute frequency was impossible to maintain, the loops could accommodate only one car at a time, and there were lengthy delays. It was obvious that the only ultimate solution was to double the track. But the Salford Council had more immediate priorities, and resolved that work on the Eccles New Road tramway should begin next, and that this should be double track ; it was also agreed to continue the Chapel Street line from its New Bailey Street junction to Blackfriars Bridge and Salford Bridge (Palatine Bridge), to connect with the Broughton route lines.

Busby and Turton, lessees of the first municipal tramway, purchased thirty vehicles from the Starbuck Company of Birkenhead. In January 1877, before services began, a specimen car was displayed on Chapel Street for the approval of councillors and members of the public. The 'knifeboard' seat was retained on the top deck, passengers facing outwards, whilst inside, longitudonal seats were placed on each side, passengers sitting with their backs to the windows

The tramway laid jointly by the Salford and Manchester town councils ran from Pendleton to Higher Broughton (Kersal Bar) by way of Deansgate and Bury New Road. The opening of the first section took place on the 17th May 1877, but services along the full length did not begin until the 30th July. Starbuck car number 29 stands in Bury New Road, Higher Broughton, ready to operate a workmen's service to Manchester. The gates of the Kersal toll bar may be seen on the left of the picture. Driver and guard now sport bowler hats. Because ladies now liked to ride on the top deck, 'decency boards' were fitted along the sides for, even with the long skirts of the period, it was not thought proper to allow glimpses of the ankle.

3
The Growth of the
Horse Tramway Network

John Eades' Reversible Tramcar

In August 1877 members of the Salford Highways Committee, whose duty it was to inspect and approve the vehicles running on the Corporation tracks, were invited to the Ford Lane, Pendleton, works of the Carriage Company to inspect two special workmen's tramcars, designed by John Eades, which were under construction there. John Eades had been born in Guide Bridge in 1841, and had come to Pendleton to enter the service of John Greenwood, junior, in 1862 as a Foreman Coachmaker. From 1867 he was the Manager of the Company's Works, in charge of maintaining, repairing and constructing omnibuses, and with the advent of tramways he assumed a position of great importance in the region.

His specially-designed workmen's cars were capable of carrying 50 persons, 22 inside and 28 outside, but his first major innovation was in a smaller vehicle for 32 passengers (16 in and 16 out) being constructed at the same time, and for which he had filed patents in June 1877. This was the Eades Patent Reversible Tramcar. The cars ordered from the Starbuck Company, seating 40, were long and heavy, with staircases at both ends, needing greater depot space and greater horse power. At the end of a

journey, the draw bar and pole had to be unfastened and shifted with the horses from one end of the car to the other. The Eades Patent Reversible Car was shorter and lighter, yet carried only eight passengers less. It required less depot space, and could be worked by a stud of eight horses, as against twelve for an ordinary car. But its big advantage was that its body, held in position by a locking pin, was able to swivel on its underframe, enabling it to be turned round at the end of a journey with the horses still in harness and with the driver remaining in his seat. It was said that such a car could reverse in four seconds. The reversible apparatus allowed the builder to dispense with the second platform, so that it was cheaper to construct, as well as offering economies in operation. The prototype was described thus : "The roof is reached by two stairs at the rear of the car, the dangerous side-step being thus dispensed with. Each axle has a compensatory wheel, enabling the car to traverse the sharp curves at street corners without grinding. The vehicle is also provided with springs which give an agreeable elasticity to the motion and reduce the jolting when any hard

continued over

his model of an Eades Patent Reversible Tramcar was made by pprentices at the Pendleton Works, and is now in the care of the Manchester Transport Museum Society. It is photographed partly turned show the swivel action of the body on the truck. The first Eades models were built with the traditional 'knifeboard' seat, but later ones had forward-facing 'garden seats,' as seen here. The ability to turn the tramcar on its truck made the second staircase unnecessary, and vehicles became shorter and lighter. *(Photo M.T.M.S.)*

substance lies on the rail. The interior of the car is airy and comfortable." After inspecting this first model, the Committee gave permission for its trial use for one week, first on the Pendleton route then on the Broughton service. A further inspection in September 1877 resulted in permission to use the car permanently, but with recommendations that on future cars the inside height of the ceiling should be raised six inches, and that the platform should be slightly enlarged. Subsequent reversible cars were consequently increased in length from 17 feet 6 inches to 22 feet, and had accommodation for 41, 18 inside and 23 on top. It was decided that the provision of twin staircases at the rear of the car was unnecessary, and future models had only one, thus allowing more space and permitting passengers to board by the side or rear of the platform step. Tramcars of this type were constructed for the Company at the Ford Lane works under Eades' personal supervision over the next two decades ; others were built under licence elsewhere and were used in many towns of the British Isles. The success of the reversible car enabled Eades to move from his modest home in Broughton Road, to Highfield Terrace, Fitzwarren Street, Pendleton, where he bought four large houses, occupying one close to Lower Seedley Road.

Plans For New Lines To Eccles

Salford Corporation, anxious to open new routes as quickly as possible, had meantime begun work on the Eccles New Road line. Manchester waited to gain experience of working the first route, and decided to double the track on the Strangeways portion of Bury New Road before embarking on new projects, suggesting that Salford should do the same on its length between the Manchester boundary and Kersal. Salford, however, had opted for additional loops at various points along the route, obviating the necessity of applying for Parliamentary powers to lay a second line. The Oldfield Road - Regent Road - Eccles New Road line as far as the Eccles boundary was inspected on the 16th January 1878 and a route from Deansgate to Ladywell along these roads opened on the following day. The section of track along Regent Road, between its junction with Oldfield Road and Regent Bridge, was inspected at the same time, but remained unused because lines on the Manchester side of Regent Bridge had not yet been laid. The additional passing loops on the Higher Broughton route were also inspected. (Busby and Turton later claimed rent reductions for the 48 days when the Bury New Road track had been out of use, firstly when Salford had been constructing the additional loops, and secondly during the doubling of the track by Manchester - the Corporation subsequently agreed this allowance.)

In November 1877, Messrs. Tahourdin and Hargreaves had applied for powers to construct a tramway from Salford to Bury, a route later included in the Manchester, Bury, Rochdale & Oldham Steam Tramway Company's plans. This was countered in January 1878 when the Manchester Suburban Tramways Company (which, in effect, was Busby, Turton, and the Carriage Company directors), submitted a scheme of their own, which would have connected with the existing line at Kersal Bar. The proposal indicated that the new line would be used for goods and minerals, as well as passengers. Tahourdin and Hargreaves claimed that the Suburban Tramways Compa-

Eades Reversible Tramcar number B3 on Bury New Road. The letter 'B' indicated that it was allocated to the Broughton Depot at Knoll Street. Other letters in use were 'P' for Pendleton and 'W' for Weaste depots. The netting under the staircase was fitted to prevent persons stepping out on the offside of the tramcar. The small letters 'S 69' and 'M 557' refer to licences granted by the Watch Committees of Salford and Manchester. (Photo courtesy C.Blood.

ny's planned double line to Bury would be of little use if through services to Manchester suffered blockages on the Salford single-track section, and that, in any event, the Company had produced the counter-proposal only to protect its monopoly. Their claim may well have been correct, as the Company's scheme was dropped in April 1878.

The tracks constructed by the Barton and Eccles Local Board, continued the Salford lines from the boundary on Eccles New Road at Ladywell to Eccles Market Place, and on through Patricroft to Peel Green. They were inspected by Major Marindin for the Board of Trade on Monday the 27th May 1878. As part of the same contract, the Board had also laid a branch from a junction at Eccles Market Place along Church Street to the Salford boundary at Gildabrook on the Eccles Old Road, in the expectation of a second route to Eccles being constructed by Salford Corporation in the near future.

Saturday, the 1st June 1878 saw the formal opening of the first Eccles lines. At 1.00 p.m. a tramcar decorated with flags, and drawn by four horses, carried Busby, Turton, and local councillors from the Board's offices to Deansgate, via Weaste and Oldfield Road, and then returned along the whole length of line to Peel Green, where the party dined at the Unicorn Inn. The local press reported that "*a most sumptuous dinner was served in the very best style of culinary art,*" and that afterwards toasts to the success of the new tramways and speeches praising the prosperity which they would bring to the Patricroft district, were made with great enthusiasm. It was clear that the local councillors looked forward with some impatience to the completion of the Salford portion of the second route to Eccles along the Old Road, but William Turton chose the occasion to sound a note of caution. He was by no means as enthusiastic about the Eccles Old Road route, had reservations about its gradients, and felt that experience of the New Road line would show that only one route to Eccles was really needed.

Although Turton was in a minority of one at these celebrations, his views were shared, for different reasons, by many residents of Eccles Old Road. A deputation opposed to the construction of another line waited upon the Local Board to make their views known, for many felt that a tramway would be detrimental to the high-class residential area. However, Salford Corporation continued to press ahead with plans, and the contract for the Eccles Old Road line was awarded to W.J.Thompson once again, the cost to be £5475. It was agreed that in constructing the new line, a junction should be laid in at Pendleton for a future line to Irlams O'Th'Height, and that a loop 'from the up to the down line' be included in front of the Woolpack Hotel 'to enable the cars to turn without changing the horses,' a reference to the Starbuck double-ended cars, at that date still a substantial portion of the fleet. The track along Eccles Old Road between Pendleton and Eccles was planned as a single line with passing loops. This was hotly debated in the Salford Council, many arguing that this was a scheme which had already been proved a failure. In reply, it was stated that the traffic along

The first tramway to Eccles was along the Eccles New Road via Weaste, reaching as far as Peel Green. It opened in June 1878. A well-patronised Eades car stands at Eccles Cross, ready to depart in the direction of Manchester. Bradburn's Eccles Cake shop may be seen on the left, and Church Street lies behind the tramcar.

the Old Road would not be very great, and although the Tramways Committee would have preferred a double line, in view of the opposition to any sort of line and to avoid inconvenience to carriages, the Corporation had been advised to keep strictly to the provisions of the plan already approved by Act of Parliament.

Contrary to the attitude of the Eccles Old Road residents, those living in Swinton and Pendlebury were anxious to know about the plans for the line from Pendleton to Irlams O'Th'Height. A petition for a tramway to Swinton was presented in June 1878, and Salford agreed to construct its section along Bolton Road as soon as the Swinton Council had gained powers to continue the tracks along Manchester Road and Chorley Road to Swinton Church in their portion beyond the boundary.

An anonymous correspondent aired the grievance in the local press :-
"*As usual, everybody and everywhere before Swinton ! Eccles, not content with her excellent service of trains and 'busses, must needs to the fore with TWO lines of tramway ; and to show how good a case their Board had, it has actually carried the Old Road scheme in the face of the bitterest opposition from the select circle of aristocratic personages who inhabit that suburban paradise. Who shall say after this that the "land o' cakes" has not shown a most commendable and plucky spirit, and deserves to reap the reward of her energy and enterprise, both financially and otherwise ? Swinton Board, please copy !*"

In the event, the Swinton Council decided not to apply for powers, but in October 1878 encouraged the Manchester Suburban Tramways Company to petition for a double track from Irlams O'Th'Height to a point opposite St. Peter's Church, Swinton. At this time, the Manchester Suburban Tramways Company was applying for powers to construct several lines in the outer suburbs of Manchester, with the intention of connecting with future city-owned lines at the boundaries, and in due course gained authority for a line from Irlams O'Th'Height to Swinton. In Salford, the Eccles Old Road line from Pendleton was under construction and was expected to be operational by Christmas 1878. In November 1878 Manchester, still debating the merits of various systems, agreed to place advertisements inviting suggestions for the kind of tramways thought suitable for laying down in the city. They received no fewer than 34 responses, including a model from John Haworth, which the sub-committee retained with a view to laying an experimental length.

Severe winter conditions held up progress on Salford's Eccles Old Road line, and the work of joining with the Eccles tracks in Gilda Brook Road was not completed until February 1879. The new line was approved in the following month, the Inspecting Officer, Major Marindin, reporting that the road was paved with "hard freestone setts, the rails being edged with a line on each side of scoria bricks." He added that the "bricks fit so exactly that a smoother and better roadway than any I have yet seen is produced." The scoria bricks, made from blast furnace slag, had been used on the orders of Arthur Jacob, Borough Engineer. Previously, Welsh setts had been used to line the edge of the earlier tracks, and they had been laid three-quarters of an inch above the level of the rails, to make allowance for wear. But, in fact, they did not wear much faster than the rails, and a number of complaints about inconvenience and damage to wheeled vehicles had been received. The new scoria bricks, said to wear well and evenly, were laid level with the rails, and complaints ceased.

Services on this second route to Eccles commenced on the day following the inspection, Wednesday the 19th March 1879, cars running from Patricroft to Manchester, via Eccles, Eccles Old Road, and Pendleton. At first, cars on both routes through Eccles terminated at the end of the double line, just beyond Patricroft Bridge, the additional length of line to Peel Green remaining unused. Although the track had been completed and used for the formal opening, contractors laying new sewers caused obstructions, and the lessees took the opportunity to work a shortened service for many months, despite protestations from the Local Board in October 1878 that the cars should use the whole of the line. Later, the Eccles New Road service did work along the full length to Peel Green, whereas the Eccles Old Road cars continued to terminate at Patricroft, except on Sundays.

A second route to Eccles opened via the Eccles Old Road in March 1879, to join with the other line at Eccles Cross. Residents along the leafy and fashionable Old Road objected to the original proposals, so the tramway was restricted to a single line with passing loops so as to avoid 'inconvenience to carriages.' Residents were promised that traffic on the tramway would be light and infrequent.

A view taken from the top deck of one tramcar shows another waiting in the passing loop on Church Street, Eccles. The date of the picture is 1892, and it was taken on a Sunday afternoon. Tramcars on the Eccles Old Road route terminated at Patricroft, whilst Eccles New Road cars travelled the full length to Peel Green.

Another view shows a tramcar at the same spot in Church Street, Eccles. This time, the car for Manchester is waiting for the Patricroft-bound car (centre distance) to arrive in the loop. Note the horse trough and stone cross to the right.

The Lessees' Dispute With the Corporation

Busby and Turton were soon in dispute with the Corporation again. By the terms of the lease with Salford, they were obliged to pay 10% per annum of the cost of construction of any lines which the Corporation saw fit to build. They objected, with some justification, to paying rental on stretches of track which they either could not use, or did not wish to use. An example of the former was the length of line in Regent Road between its junction with Oldfield Road and Regent Bridge, which had lain unused because Manchester had not yet constructed tracks within its city limits from Regent Bridge onwards to Deansgate. When this had been done, the lessees argued, they could provide an additional route into Manchester which would relieve congestion on Chapel Street, but until then the line was of no use to them. (In fact, the lessees paid rent on this stretch of track for almost two years until Manchester made the connection at Regent Bridge in December 1880.) Likewise, they urged the Corporation not to proceed with the Blackfriars extension, which they said would be used by only 1% of the passengers. As a minor irritation, they drew attention to the 'inconvenience' caused by the Fire Brigade laying water hoses across the track. The Council remained unmoved by their pleas, and W.J.Thompson was awarded the contract for a double-track extension from Chapel Street to Blackfriars. The lessees were also unhappy about certain clauses proposed in the local byelaws governing the operation of tramway carriages. Busby, Turton and the Carriage Company suggested that "persons who are likely to be a nuisance are not to be allowed to ride inside a car." The Council proposed an even sterner amendment, and wanted to extend this suggestion to exclude potential nuisances from the "outside" (i.e. the open top) also. In this respect, it appeared that the 'nuisances' referred to were dirty-clothed workmen, who, it was believed, would be likely to offend ladies who now often rode on the top deck. The Salford Town Clerk appealed to the Board of Trade in support of the Council's proposed exclusion clause - he wrote that the population of Salford was now "very mixed" and that the tramways now extended into the rural parts, where, he argued, it was "not unusual for females in holiday attire to prefer the outside of the car to the inside." The Board of Trade agreed. When eventually approved, the byelaws contained some regulations which it must have been difficult to follow, and others which must have been impossible to check. Responsibility for the observance of some of the byelaws was placed on the conductor or driver - for example, potential passengers wearing 'offensive clothing' or suffering from a 'contagious disease,' were not to be carried. No carriage was supposed to average a speed of less than five miles per hour or more than eight, and no carriage was to drive less than 30 yards behind a preceding one. There was to be no performing on musical instruments ! The byelaws also included clauses relating to the crew of the horse trams. Drivers had to be over 21 and conductors over 16; employees were to be sober at all times, and were not to 'wilfully deceive' passengers as to the route.

The crews were responsible for the conduct of their business, and any failures could be punished by either the Company or the civic authorities. A guard on a Chapel Street tramcar, for example, was reported by a police constable for carrying seven more than the permitted number of passengers, and was subsequently fined twenty shillings in court.

By the time of the publication of the byelaws, Busby and Turton's contract with the Carriage Company was well-known, and the partners had tried without success to have their lease formally transferred to the Company. The Corporations of Manchester and Salford claimed, however, that under the terms of their agreements there should have been no sub-letting to the Company unless the two Councils had first been properly consulted and had given their approval. Press opinion supported the stance of the two Corporations, and hinted at some sinister motive behind the desire to transfer the lease. One editorial suggested that if the lease was to be transferred, the annual rental for the lines should increase from 10% to 12% of the cost of construction. Other criticisms included the alleged failure of the Carriage Company to run the early morning workmen's cars, and the Company's resistance to the introduction of short-distance fares. In an atmosphere of mutual distrust, the civic authorities announced that the transfer of the lease would not be contemplated until all the planned lines had been completed.

A share certificate of the Manchester Carriage Company, dated 1879, and signed by John Greenwood (Junior) as one of the directors.

Although Eades reversible cars were constructed in large numbers and formed the bulk of the fleet, the original Starbuck cars remained in use for workmen's services and various short workings. Here, a double-ended Starbuck car, number P 20, is seen on Eccles New Road allocated to the Weaste route.

The Tramways To Swinton And Lower Broughton

In the meantime, the Borough Engineer had prepared plans for the proposed line to Irlams O'Th'Height, and had recommended to the Council that other lines authorised in the 1875 Salford Tramways and Improvements Act should be begun in the near future, as powers to construct them would expire in June 1880. Subsequently, it was agreed to dispense with the projected lines in Cross Lane and the Blackfriars to Salford Bridge length in Lower Chapel Street, but to push ahead with the route to Lower Broughton via Blackfriars Road, Great Clowes Street, and Lower Broughton Road. A suggested link with the Bury New Road line from Great Clowes Street was opposed by Busby and Turton, as not likely to be profitable in competition with the existing route to Higher Broughton. It could be worked only at a "ruinous loss," they said. The idea was later dropped. It was agreed that the Bolton Road line to Irlams O'Th'Height should be double-track, and the contract for this and the Lower Broughton line was awarded to Messrs. Evans & Lewin, a move to give the work to Thompson being defeated. Manchester Corporation was asked to proceed with their portion of the Blackfriars Street track.

The additional length of double track along Chapel Street to Blackfriars was ready by the end of February 1880, and though inspected and approved, remained unused by the lessees. The section from Pendleton to Irlams O'Th'Height, double track throughout, was inspected on the Wednesday, the 12th May 1880. William Barningham & Company Limited, of Pendleton Ironworks on Strawberry Road, had supplied the rails. Opposite the Packhorse Inn at Irlams O'Th'Height, the lines joined end-on with those constructed by the Manchester Suburban Tramways Company to Swinton, which were to be inspected at the same time, and the official party, which included William Turton (described as Chairman of the Leeds Tramways), Greenwood, Eades, and Robert Guest (local manager for the Company), left Pendleton on a special car at 10.55 a.m. to accompany Major General Hutchinson to Swinton. Public services began instantly approval had been gained, the first service car leaving Pendleton for Swinton at 12.45 p.m. Thereafter a 30 minute frequency was maintained. Cars on the new route from Irlams O'Th'Height and Swinton entered Manchester via New Bailey Street, but returned using only the outward track of the new lines in Blackfriars Street and Chapel Street.

The Pendlebury Fare Dispute

The fare on the tramcar from Swinton to Manchester was 4d in 3d out, from Pendleton 3d in 2d out, as had obtained on the omnibuses, and for the convenience of Pendlebury passengers a horse bus ran every hour to and from the junction with the new tramway at Irlams O'Th'Height, first at a standard fare of twopence, immediately reduced, after vociferous protests, to one penny. Pendlebury residents were outraged. A spokesman said they were being treated "like a gang of colliers, below the consideration of the Carriage Company." Lacking the convenience of a tramway, and having now lost their through omnibus service to Pendleton, they objected that they now had to pay more for the same journey. Paying to arrive by omnibus at Irlams O'Th'Height, on changing to the tramcar they were charged the full fare as if they had journeyed from Swinton. A Swinton resident travelling to Manchester could thus make the through journey at a lower fare than a Pendlebury passenger, who was forced to change vehicles and pay twice. A protest meeting was held, and it was claimed that many Pendlebury residents now preferred to walk to the railway station at Clifton Junction, from where they could obtain a return ticket to Manchester for 9d, which was a penny less than the tram-plus-omnibus return fare.

Before the tramway to Irlams O'Th'Height had opened, travellers from Pendlebury had changed vehicles at Pendleton, from where the services to Manchester were more frequent. Now, it was claimed, they had to wait up to twenty minutes at The Height, where there was no shelter, unless one entered the public house. The Manchester Suburban Tramways Act of 1879 provided that fares from Swinton and Pendlebury to Manchester should not exceed 4d in 3d out, and the objectors thought they had a valid point in demonstrating that the combined omnibus and tramcar journey from Pendlebury was one penny more than this stipulated figure. However, the Company's response was to declare that they were not legally bound to run the connecting omnibus at all. In fact, the officials at the meeting threatened to withdraw it, because, they claimed, the Company was losing some £10 per week on the service. The Swinton Local Board took advice, and discovered that, although the Tramways Company and the Carriage Company were 'practically the same,' legally they were two different bodies, and the agreement was with the Tramways Company only. Suitably chastened, local councillors asked if the Company would lease a single line

Residents of Pendlebury did not gain a tramway until 1898. Until then, they had to change from tramcar to horse-drawn omnibus at Irlams O'Th'Height, and pay more for the privilege. An omnibus for Pendlebury passengers waits in Bolton Road for the tramcar from Pendleton to arrive.

Nº 2193

William Barningham and Company, Limited.

PENDLETON IRON WORKS, PENDLETON, MANCHESTER.

CAPITAL £60,000, IN 3,000 SHARES OF £20 EACH.

REGISTERED 2nd NOVEMBER 1874.

SHARE CERTIFICATE.

This is to Certify that *Simon Horrocks,* of *Pendlebury, near Manchester, Colliery Manager,* is the Proprietor of the Share No. 2193 of the Company called

WILLIAM BARNINGHAM AND COMPANY, LIMITED,

subject to the Conditions and Regulations of the Company.

Given under the Common Seal of the said Company, and signed by two Directors and countersigned by the Secretary, this Ninth day of November 1874.

Signed _James Burford_
_____ } Two Directors.

Countersigned _Alf Bowes_ Secretary.

N.B.—No Transfer of the Share represented by this Certificate will be Registered until such Transfer has been deposited in the Office of the Company.

(below). Salford Corporation constructed the tramway from Pendleton to the municipal boundary at Irlams O'Th'Height, and the Carriage Company continued the line for the Swinton Urban District Council as far as Swinton Church in 1880. An Eades car stands at the end of the line at Swinton opposite the church near the Bull's Head Hotel, having turned ready to resume its inward journey.

The company of William Barningham, with works on Strawberry Road, Pendleton, supplied the rails for the construction of the tramway to Irlams O'Th'Height

to Pendlebury if the Local Board constructed it. The Company replied that they saw "no prospect of the line proving remunerative."

The dispute gave added impetus to the argument for short-distance fares, and correspondents pointed to the example set by Glasgow, but to no avail. A complaint of a different character emanated from a number of Pendleton shopkeepers. They protested bitterly about the loss of trade now that Pendlebury passengers no longer changed vehicles outside their premises. There were complaints, too, about the slow speed of the tramcars. Several objectors claimed that it could take up to thirty minutes to travel from Pendleton to Manchester. Others suggested that steam power should replace the horses to give a more rapid service. One correspondent claimed that "the drivers give one the impression that they learnt their art at funerals."

Trouble sometimes emanated from within the Company. The Directors must have been alarmed to read a prominent press article under the headline 'Anti-Moustache Movement,' in which it was revealed that a Company official had ordered guards to improve their appearance by shaving off moustaches, threatening dismissal for those who failed to comply. The Directors promptly distanced themselves from this conflict, and announced that the order had been without their authorisation, and that they did not approve.

The 'Opposition Bus' To Pendlebury

The lack of a through route to Pendlebury gave rise to an unusual form of competition. On the 4th June 1880, a rival service began between Manchester and the Windmill Hotel, Pendlebury, the fare being 4d inside, 3d on top. The new omnibus ran only two or three times per day, with extra journeys on Saturdays, and this was thought to be insufficient. The vehicle used was described as Wood's Patent Tram-Bus. Locally, it was named the 'Opposition Bus.' In its construction, it was reminiscent of Haworth's 1861 tramway vehicles, in that it operated on the on-and-off principle and made use of guide wheels to enable it to travel on the tramway wherever possible. Wood's omnibus had the usual four wheels, but each pair was set at such a distance apart as to be able to fit exactly upon the smooth outer surface of the tram rails. Inside the front wheels, were two smaller ones, which the driver could raise or lower by means of a lever. When the omnibus joined the tramway, the driver positioned the large wheels on the smooth surface of the rails, and lowered the two small ones into the rail grooves. The front wheels of the omnibus, unlike the tramcars, had a swivel action to enable the driver to manoeuvre it on and off the lines, and it was said that when on the tramway it ran as smoothly and as silently as the trams. When off the lines, however, the iron guide wheels sometimes trailed along the stone setts and made a great noise. When travelling from Pendlebury, the 'Opposition Bus' joined the tramway at Irlams O'Th'Height and followed it through Pendleton to Manchester. It had also been noted operating on lines in Eccles.

A protest was made to Salford Town Council by the Carriage Company on behalf of Busby and Turton, claiming that the lessees, had exclusive use of the tramway, but the Town Clerk informed John Greenwood that the lessees must initiate their own action to stop the nuisance. Consequently, Mr. Robert Guest, Manager of the Company's Pendleton Office, travelled on the 'Opposition Bus' on the 9th June 1880 to collect evidence. He journeyed from the Woolpack Hotel, Pendleton, as far as Irlams O'Th'Height, and noticed that the driver used the tramway as much as possible, whilst a conductor collected fares in the usual way. He warned the driver, Thomas Cottam, that in running a vehicle with wheels specially made to fit the tram rails, he was in contravention of the Tramways Act and liable to a fine of several pounds. Cottam's response, according to the local newspaper, was "Make it a thousand ! Gee up !"

As a result, Cottam was summoned by Busby and Turton to appear before the magistrates at Salford Borough Police Court on the 23rd June 1880, charged with unlawfully using a tramway with an omnibus specially made for that purpose. Cottam admitted that he used the tram rails, but argued that the vehicle was not so constructed as to be used only on a tramway, and that therefore he was not infringing the Tramways Act. He claimed that there was no law to prevent any other vehicle from running upon the lines. The magistrates decided that Wood's vehicle had been constructed with the deliberate intention of using the tramlines, and the defendant was fined forty shillings. The demise of his service was evidently not mourned by Pendlebury residents - the local press described the vehicle as a "most detestable nuisance" and claimed that most people preferred to walk to Swinton or The Height to meet the tramcar rather than suffer the noise of Wood's omnibus. "If they are to suffer, they prefer it should be peaceably," ended an editorial.

A local tradesman, Mr.Barrett, achieved popularity by publishing a series of cartoons showing Pendlebury people travelling to Manchester by a number of bizarre methods, including balloon flights.

Another, less bizarre, 'pirate' horse-drawn omnibus ran regular services from Seedley to Manchester, via Ellor Street, successfully tapping a source of passengers not catered for by the tramways to Weaste and Pendleton.

Sunday Tramcar Services

The provision of Sunday tramcar services did not meet with universal approval in 1880. Members of the Barton and Eccles Local Board complained that Sunday tramcars were "a serious nuisance to places of worship." The cars were too frequent and too well-patronised, it was said, and church attendances had fallen as a result. Because of similar opposition, there were no Sunday services on the Swinton route at first, though the lessees said they would provide them if there was a demand. Some seven weeks after the opening of the Swinton route, the local council voted by a narrow majority to request a Sunday service, which began to run hourly (afternoons only) on the 4th July 1880. However, to avoid distracting churchgoers at St.Peter's, the trams stopped short, some quarter of a mile before the usual terminus outside the church, and terminated instead at Swinton Market Place.

This practice gave rise to an unusual method of working. The double track from the Salford boundary had been laid without any cross-over points. Consequently, a tramcar reversing at Swinton Market Place was unable to change to the inward track, and so travelled back to Irlams O'Th'Height on the wrong side of the road until it was able to regain its correct position via the cross-over in Bolton Road at Irlams O'Th'Height.

The early morning workmen's car from Swinton at 5.00 a.m. (fare twopence, inside or out) followed a similar procedure, the Company alleging that no workmen resided beyond the Market Place.

The Manchester Carriage & Tramways Company 1880

By an Act of the 2nd August 1880 the Manchester Carriage Company was merged with the Manchester Suburban Tramways Company to form the Manchester Carriage and Tramways Company. The Boards of Directors of the two former companies had comprised mainly the same people, and the first directors of the new Company were the existing directors of the Carriage Company. The Act transferred to the new Company all the powers gained in the Manchester Suburban Tramways Acts and Orders, though the original lease of the first lines remained officially with Busby and Turton alone. The ownership or lease of all other lines already in existence, plus those yet to be constructed, was vested in the new Company, whose empire was destined to extend as far as Ashton, Cheetham Hill, Denton, Oldham, Stalybridge, Stockport, and Stretford. The year 1880 was the peak period for horse-tramway construction in the region, and services were operated over some 75 miles of track, of which 25 miles were owned by the Company, 28 miles were leased from Manchester Corporation, 13 from Salford, and various shorter lengths from several Local Boards, including Barton and Eccles. By the middle of the year, the Company operated 108 tramcars on routes already opened, another 53 cars were ready for the commencement of new routes, and 22 more were under construction in the carriage building department of the Pendleton Works.

The line to Lower Broughton, a mixture of double track with single-line and passing loops (because of road-width restrictions on parts of the route), was completed and inspected on the 10th September 1880. It terminated in a dual stub-end at 'The Cliff,' a point on Lower Broughton Road beyond Cromwell Bridge, known as 'Broughton Spout,' opposite the end of Laurel Grove. The contractors, Evans and Lewin, were said to have made no profit on the construction of the line because of the great number of points (22) and passing loops on this route. Major General Hutchinson took the opportunity to recommend the provision of an additional brake at the rear end of the Eades reversible cars, which request was duly passed on by the Council to the lessees. All authorised lines in Salford, except those for which plans had been dropped, were thus complete, and the system settled down to a period of consolidation.

The dispute over the transfer of the original lease rumbled on, the Council taking every opportunity to record possible infringements or failures on the part of the operators to meet requirements. The request for additional brake power had been prompted by experience of working the long gradients on the Bury New Road line to Higher Broughton, and although the lessees had promised to act on the inspector's recommendation, nothing had been done. The lessees likewise failed to keep promises to run workmen's cars on the Lower Broughton route, or to run service cars on the Blackfriars section. In respect of Lower Broughton, they claimed that workmen's cars would be useless, as this was "not a district where working men reside." As to the Blackfriars section of track, they pointed out that it was used as a 'return loop' for cars which had entered Manchester via New Bailey Street, but reminded the Council that it was "laid down against the wishes of the lessees," that very few passengers wished to use that length of track, that the steep gradient in Blackfriars Street was not good for incoming cars, and that confusion would result if inward cars alternated between the two routes.

John Greenwood, Junior, had been elected to represent Seedley Ward as a Liberal member of Salford Borough Council in 1878, and so was instantly accessible to answer queries about the tramway services. However, as an interested party, he was careful to play no part whatsoever in the negotiations for the transfer of the lease, for which purpose a special sub-committee had been set up. An interview with Busby and Turton was arranged for June 1881, and it was made clear to the lessees that the transfer would be dependent upon their being willing to attend to the previous complaints, and to consider the introduction of children's and short-distance fares. By September, at a second meeting, Busby was ready to concede all points except that concerning the short-distance fares. He declared that if short-stage fares were to be introduced on the Salford lines, then the Company would have to do likewise on all their other routes in the Manchester area, and this would mean that the transfer of the lease would be dearly bought. Neither side would give way, and the battle for the transfer of the lease and

the campaign for penny fares was to continue over a number of years.

The Higher Broughton (Kersal) to Bury standard gauge section of the Manchester, Bury, Rochdale and Oldham Steam Tramways Company was inspected and approved on the 21st February 1883. The Company began operation on Monday, the 12th March at 9.00 a.m., when two engines and cars cars set off from Bury (Derby Hotel) to travel the six miles to Kersal. The first service car ran at 11.00 a.m., and there were five return trips on the first day. It was not possible to increase the service because the tracks in Bury were not yet connected to the depot for access to the rest of the rolling stock, but on the second day ten trips were operated on the delivery of a third engine direct from the railway goods station. After the first week, there were still six engines and cars isolated in the depot, and the service was said to be erratic. At the Bury end, the Company had lines on two different gauges, with mixed-gauge track in the town centre.

A proposed end-on connection with the Salford lines at Kersal Bar, and a siding to facilitate the transfer of passengers from the steam to the horse trams was opposed by the Carriage & Tramways Company, whose officials were encouraged by the number of complaints from residents near the Moor Lane and Singleton Road junctions about the annoyances caused by the steam-tram locomotives in blocking the road, dropping oil and grease on the surface, and emitting foul smoke. Indeed, in February 1884 the Steam Tramways Company was fined £2 at Salford Magistrates' Court for making a 'clatter' through their failure to keep locomotives at the Kersal terminus in good repair, and the M.B.R.O. sought to relieve the Kersal residents by

The Manchester, Bury, Rochdale & Oldham Steam Tramway Company opened a line from Bury via Prestwich to Higher Broughton in 1883, though the service was later cut-back to run only as far as Whitefield.

Box-like steam locomotive number 41, hauling a passenger trailer, is pictured here in Manchester Road, Bury, outside the Pack Horse Hotel, on its way to Whitefield about 1899.

seeking access via the Salford tracks to a terminus at Blackfriars Bridge. The Borough Council referred the Company to the existing lessees of the lines, who, of course, resisted the proposal and insisted on their exclusive right to work the lines into Manchester. Elsewhere in the city, the Carriage & Tramways Company was itself the target of criticisms, mainly concerning slow and infrequent services, which culminated in mid-June 1883, when tramcars were removed from their regular routes to take advantage of the exceptional traffic to Manchester Racecourse. The Racecourse at that time was located on the New Barns Estate, near Trafford Road, where the Chief Constable had previously urged the construction of a new line in Goodiers Lane and Trafford Road to cater for the crowds of racegoers, and to avoid delay and obstruction to traffic in Regent Road and Eccles New Road. His suggestion could not be acted upon immediately, as a new authorising Act would have been required, but it was incorporated into a later Provisional Order.

Early in 1884 the Mayor of Salford, accompanied by the Town Clerk, Borough Surveyor, and two council members, attended a meeting at the Market Street office of the Carriage Company to discuss the proposed doubling of the Bury New Road line. The lessees were in favour, but did not wish to pay an additional rent, for, they argued, whilst doubling the track would be an advantage, it would not mean any increase in receipts. The occasion afforded another opportunity to present several criticisms of the services provided by the Company - these included once again the lack of workmen's cars on the Lower Broughton route, the irregularity of running on Eccles New Road, and the suspension of services during race meetings. Another item raised which was the source of much discontent was that of advertising on the tramcars. Earlier the Council had agreed to advertising panels being placed inside tramcars, subject to the approval of a committee. The lessees had disputed the Council's right to supervise this matter, and claimed that no other authority interpreted the regulations in the way Salford did. Consequently, they had proceeded to fix advertisements inside the cars without reference to the Authority. The Council now ordered them to be removed, and threatened legal action if the lessees did not comply. At a more conciliatory meeting in September, Busby's offer to remove existing advertisements as the contracts expired, and to submit new ones for approval, was accepted.

Proposed Additions To The System

A Provisional Board of Trade Order was sought late in 1884 for permission to construct additional lengths of track, as under :-

Bury New Road - doubling of the track between Moor Lane and the Manchester boundary at the Grove Inn ; and a short length to connect with the M.B.R.O. lines at Kersal.

Lower Broughton Road - Camp Street to Broughton Bridge. (The existing 1880 lines reached Lower Broughton via Great Clowes Street and Broughton Lane).

Cross Lane and Trafford Road (later withdrawn because of an objection from the London & North Western Railway Company about Cross Lane bridge).

Goodiers Lane - a loop for race traffic from Regent Road, returning via Trafford Road. (A proposal for a further length to the Racecourse gates in Broadway was withdrawn because of fears of obstruction to carriages and possible congestion at the entrance gates.)

SEE MAP ON PAGE 26

The nine objectors to the above proposals included the lessees (because they wanted to be consulted about additional tracks on which they would have to pay rent), the railway company, and several residents. A siding in Heyworth Street, at the side of the Company's Weaste Depot in Eccles New Road (Derby Road corner) was laid by the lessees themselves, though the Council insisted that it must be regarded only as a "temporary stand on occasions of extraordinary traffic." The siding turned out from a loop in front of the depot premises, and was obviously useful in offering a side entrance to the stables and shed, as well as removing short-working vehicles out of the way of the through service cars to and from Eccles. Even so, there were Council complaints that cars were standing too long on the siding.

At this period, the Council revived the complaints about the inadequate brake power on the tramcars, and their case was supported by a potentially serious incident on the Bury New Road gradient above the Grove Inn. The brake on a heavily-loaded car 'became fractured or otherwise inoperative,'

and it was reported that the tramcar 'shot down the slope at great speed' to the danger of the passengers. The Borough Engineer was directed to find out whether the Board Of Trade recommendation about the fitting of double brakes had been carried out by the lessees, but it is almost certain that the councillors were well aware that nothing had been done.

Death Of John Greenwood, Junior, 1886

John Greenwood, Junior, resigned from the Salford Borough Council in 1884, but remained Chairman of the Manchester Carriage and Tramways Company, though described as a 'retired omnibus proprietor.' He died at his home, Bolton Lodge, near Eccles, on the 21st March 1886, aged 67. He was survived by his wife, Helen, four daughters, and one son, also John, then aged 30, a mining engineer, though later he, too, worked for the Company and eventually succeeded to its Chairmanship. The three John Greenwoods had given rise to a local rhyme in Pendleton about "Owd John, and Young John, and Young John's son," and a newspaper obituary notice for 'Young John' began, "There was John Greenwood, and John Greenwood, and John Greenwood .....," and proceeded to draw comparisons between 'Owd John' and 'Young John.' It was evident that 'Young John' had been highly respected by both employees and business associates, a generous supporter of local charities, and generally a kind and genial man, who had been seen as the 'life and soul' of the Carriage Company. In earlier years he had been connected with the Bethesda Sunday School, in Broad Street, Pendleton, but since moving to Bolton Lodge he had attended Eccles Parish Church. He was buried in the family grave in St.John's Churchyard, Irlams O'Th'Height, the funeral being attended by many employees and past-employees, as well as civic dignitaries and directors of the Company.

The Campaign For Short-Distance Fares And The Transfer Of The Lease

Shortly after Greenwood's death the lessees of the tramways met with a Salford sub-committee and agreement was reached on the proposed additions to the track. The lessees promised to carry children under 12 for half-fare inside, and in return asked for approval for advertisement panels both inside and outside the cars. The sub-committee agreed to recommend the transfer of the lease if half-fares were to apply to both inside and outside child passengers, but would approve only inside advertising, subject to supervision. However, at a meeting of the full Council, a reduction in adult fares was demanded before approval was given for any advertising at all. The Steam Tramways Company had already introduced penny fares, and the fact that his brother William was a director of that Company, must have been an embarrassment to Daniel Busby, but a powerful argument for the Council.

The Goodiers Lane - Trafford Road loop line for race traffic was inspected by Major General Hutchinson on the 1st June 1886. Though it was to be used only occasionally, the Inspecting Officer pointed out that the Kincaid method of construction had now been abandoned by other authorities, as not standing up to heavy wear and tear, and that the Corporation should be aware that this construction would now be objected to for regular traffic. The Goodiers Lane track was used for the first time on the 14th June during the Whitsun Race Meeting, by which time work on the doubling of the Bury New Road lines was about to start. The lessees refused to run omnibuses during the reconstruction work, so a system of temporary sidings and passing places was adopted. The work of doubling the Bury New Road track and building the short length to connect with the steam tramway was completed in March 1887.

The Steam Tramway Company next announced a modest increase of fares on their route from Bury to Higher Broughton, because, they said, all their cars were to have cushions inside ! Their tramcars, which were trailers behind a steam locomotive, had unglazed top-deck covers, offering some protection from the weather. Sample fares on the steam trams were : Kersal to Prestwich, 1½d inside, 1d on top ; Kersal to Whitefield, 2½d inside, 2d on top ; Kersal to Bury, 4½d inside, 4d on top. The fare increase did not prevent the Company going into liquidation in October 1887, but a new management dropped 'Manchester' from the title, which place they had never reached anyway, and reconstituted the undertaking as 'The Bury, Rochdale & Oldham Steam Tramway Company.'

On the horse trams in 1887, the minimum inside fare was 3d, but faced with some unexpected competition from 'penny jiggers' and waggonettes, the Company reduced to 2d the fare for inside passengers travelling only half the journey.

Continued on page 27

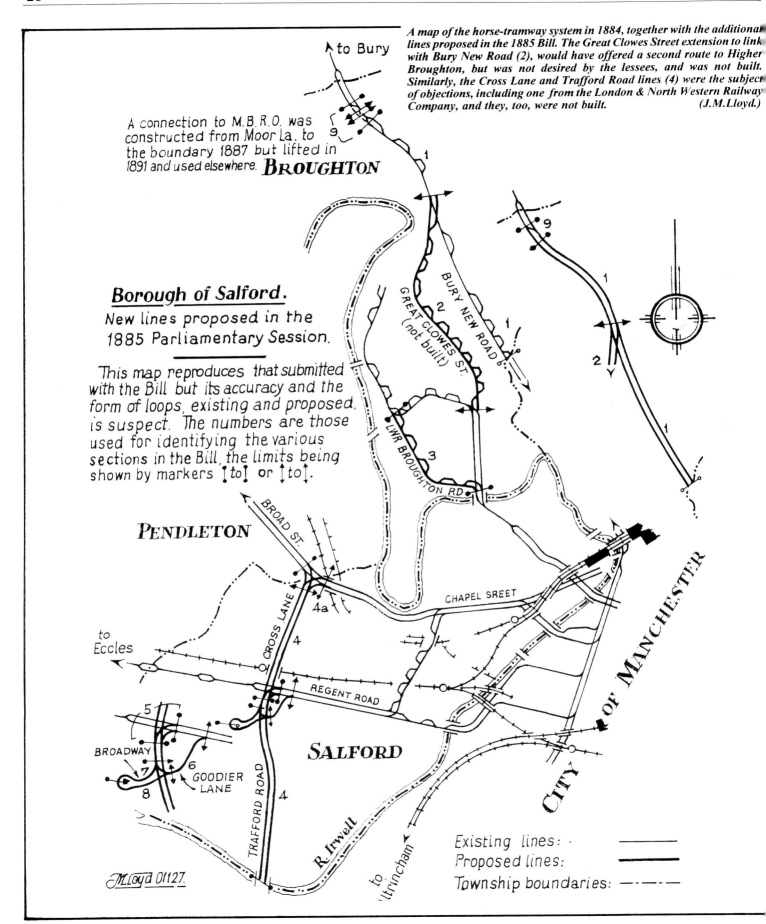

to Bury

A map of the horse-tramway system in 1884, together with the additional lines proposed in the 1885 Bill. The Great Clowes Street extension to link with Bury New Road (2), would have offered a second route to Higher Broughton, but was not desired by the lessees, and was not built. Similarly, the Cross Lane and Trafford Road lines (4) were the subject of objections, including one from the London & North Western Railway Company, and they, too, were not built. (J.M.Lloyd.)

A connection to M.B.R.O. was constructed from Moor La. to the boundary 1887 but lifted in 1891 and used elsewhere. **BROUGHTON**

Borough of Salford.

New lines proposed in the 1885 Parliamentary Session.

This map reproduces that submitted with the Bill but its accuracy and the form of loops, existing and proposed, is suspect. The numbers are those used for identifying the various sections in the Bill, the limits being shown by markers [to] or ↕to↕.

BURY NEW ROAD

GREAT CLOWES ST. (not built)

LWR BROUGHTON RD.

PENDLETON

BROAD ST.

CROSS LANE

CHAPEL SREET

to Eccles

REGENT ROAD

SALFORD

BROADWAY

GOODIER LANE

TRAFFORD ROAD

R. Irwell

to Altrincham

CITY OF MANCHESTER

M.Loyd 01127.

Existing lines: ———
Proposed lines: ━━━
Township boundaries: —·—·—

Continued from page 25

The additional lines to Lower Broughton were completed in August 1887. For these new lines, and for subsequent re-laying of worn parts of track on the Pendleton and Eccles New Road routes, iron rails of a different section, faced with steel, were used, and fixed on a more secure base, according to a system developed by Mr.Jacob. In the following year, the Company introduced short distance fares, with a minimum of 2d inside, 1d out. The requirements for the transfer of the lease had now been met, and John Greenwood (the third) was able to display, and gain approval for, a number of exterior advertisement panels, whilst negotiations were in progress. Unhappily, Daniel Busby had died in 1887, ending 18 years partnership with William Turton, and with the transfer arrangements still incomplete. The formalities were concluded in 1890. All the planned Salford lines had been included in the original agreement with Busby and Turton, which was to last for 21 years from the 31st May 1877, and the transferred lease to the Company retained the same expiry date in 1898.

In 1891 the Corporation approved a double line of rails to approach the Company's new depot in Lower Broughton Road. These new buildings became the fourth set of depot premises and stables owned by the Company in Salford, the others being at Higher Broughton (Knoll Street) ; Pendleton (Church Street) ; and Weaste (Eccles New Road/Derby Road), this latter having had its stables and tramcar shed extended in a second phase of building by March 1891. There was, in addition, the main works in Ford Lane, Pendleton. The re-laying of worn sections of track on the Pendleton and Regent Road routes continued. The rails from the short length of track on Bury New Road, from Moor Lane to the Prestwich boundary, which had been built in 1887 to connect with the steam tramway, had remained unused, and it was agreed to remove them to use elsewhere. The Kersal section of the steam tram route from Bury had proved unprofitable to the operators, and the track through Prestwich had been abandoned late in 1888, the service then running from Bury only as far as the Besses O'Th'Barn junction. In 1891 the route was further cut-back, and the steam trams operated only the 30-minute journey as far as Whitefield railway station. In the following year the service was further curtailed to run from Bury only as far as the Whitefield boundary.

Waggonettes offered competition to the horse-trams and led to a reduction in fares. This one, operated by Joseph Alexander, of Great Clowes Street, Lower Broughton, appears to be on a special outing, possibly from some local hostelry.

At this period the horse tram system was substantially complete. By 1890 the Manchester Carriage & Tramways Company had incurred capital expenditure of some £204,979 on the 25 miles of track it owned in the various districts around Manchester ; Manchester Corporation itself had spent £126,871 ; and Salford £127,572. In addition, the Company invested some £65,640 on 385 tramcars (82 of which were used on Salford routes) and £97,000 on 3583 horses (787 of which worked on the Salford lines). The working expenses of the Company totalled some £241,895 per annum, and annual receipts amounted to £331,353, about £69,000 being from the Salford routes. Its stock of both horses and tramcars grew as services increased. In 1891 the Company owned 424 tramcars and 4716 horses. Some twenty or so new tramcars to add to the fleet were constructed each year at the Pendleton Works, and as the 'garden seat' type of tramcar (i.e. with fixed forward-facing seats on the top deck) had become more popular, old 'knifeboard' seat cars were converted as they went into the Works for overhaul or repair. By the end of the century the tramcar fleet totalled 519 and the number of horses 5209.

The services operated in the Salford area in the 1890s were as listed below. At night, the cars displayed a coloured light to indicate which route they were following, and these are given, where known, together with the frequency of operation during the main part of the day. Fares given are for the full journey.

BROUGHTON, HIGHER (Red light) : From Deansgate every 7½ minutes, 8.30 a.m. to 11.00 p.m. Short workings to Great Cheetham Street. Fares 3d and 2d.

Continued on page 29

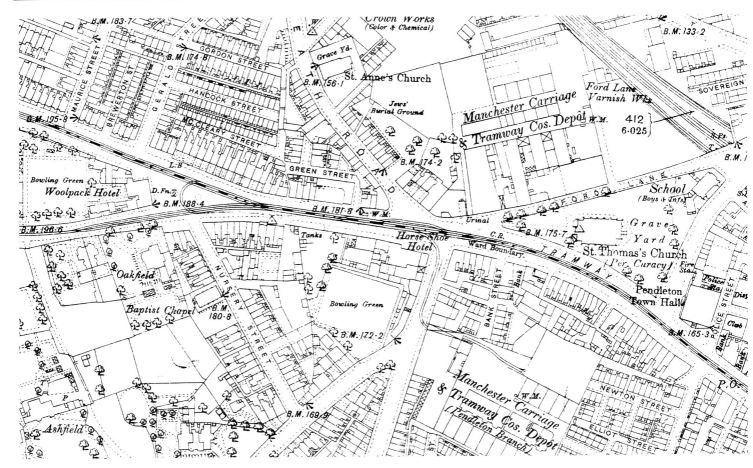

A section of the 1893 Ordnance Survey map of Pendleton shows the location of the Ford Lane Works in relation to the depot and stables in Church Street opposite. The three-track layout at Pendleton and the turning circle at the Woolpack Hotel were continued in the electric tramcar days. The toll gates at each side of the Woolpack Hotel were dismantled about 1870. The Horse Shoe Hotel, on the corner of Churc Street, of which John Greenwood (senior) was once the proprietor, wa ideally situated for supervision of the traffic at this busy junction. Joh Eades, Manager of the Pendleton Works, bought a house in Fitzwarre Street, just off the bottom left corner of the map.

The horse-tram depot and stables a Weaste were situated on Eccles Ne Road, near the corner of Derby Road A side-entrance with connecting trac was added in Heyworth Street, th location of this photograph. At on time, crew members were required t appear with clean white collar an bowler hat. The car is one allocated t the short route between Deansgate an Cross Lane, via Regent Road, thoug the 'WEASTE' destination board ha been clipped over its usual sign. Th small notice in the front window read : 'This car will not stop between Dawso Street and Regent Road Bridge an between West Craven Street, Regen Road, and Trafford Road.'

Continued from page 27

BROUGHTON, LOWER (Red light) : From Blackfriars Street every few minutes, 7.45 a.m. to 11.00 p.m. Fares 2d. in or out.
One-horse single-deck cars to and from Sussex Street every few minutes, fare 1d.

CROSS LANE via REGENT ROAD (Red light) : From Deansgate every few minutes, 7.40 a.m. to 11.15 p.m. Fare 1d. in or out.

IRLAMS O'TH'HEIGHT (Green light) : From Blackfriars Street. Extra cars morning and evening supplemented those on the SWINTON route. Fares 3d. in 2d. out.

PATRICROFT via ECCLES OLD ROAD (Green and red light) : From Blackfriars Street every 30 minutes, 9.00 a.m. to 9.00 p.m. Fare 4d. in or out.

PEEL GREEN via OLDFIELD ROAD and ECCLES NEW ROAD : From Deansgate every 30 minutes, 8.45 a.m. to 8.45 p.m. Fare 4d.

PENDLETON (Green light) : From Deansgate every few minutes, 8.00 a.m. to 11.06 p.m.

SWINTON (Orange and red light) : From Blackfriars Street every 30 minutes, 8.00 a.m. to 10.00 p.m. Fares 4d. in 3d. out.

WEASTE via LIVERPOOL ROAD and REGENT ROAD (White light) : From Deansgate every 6 minutes, 8.00 a.m. to 11.15 p.m. Fare 2d. in or out. (Another route to Weaste was via the Peel Green cars along Chapel Street and Oldfield Road.)

In addition to its tramway operation, the Company continued with its private hire and cab business, and provided omnibus services in many areas where it had not been thought worthwhile to construct a tramway, as, for example, to Pendlebury, whose residents had failed to persuade either the Company or the Council to lay tracks along Bolton Road. The omnibus network was often supplemented by services offered by smaller independent proprietors, usually in the more sparsely populated districts, and sometimes connecting with the tramway. An example was the waggonette run by Samuel Hooley between Patricroft and Irlam. In 1891 it is recorded as operating on only three days per week, Mondays, Wednesdays and Saturdays, making four journeys each way, at a through fare of fourpence, with penny stages in between. There was likewise a regular omnibus service between the Stocks Hotel at Walkden and Farnworth.

Despite its continued growth, the 1890s were to prove an anxious decade for the Carriage and Tramways Company, as the date for the expiration of the leases approached, and the threat of a municipal take-over grew more real.

In addition to its tramcar services, the Manchester Carriage Company continued to provide vehicles for private hire work. Hansom cab number 100, for two passengers, has the Company title and its charges painted on the exterior, ninepence per mile, two shillings per hour.

The original Stocks Hotel at Walkden was a staging post, with extensive stables at the rear. This second hotel built on the site remained an important interchange point for connecting services. The horse-bu operated between Walkden and Farnworth, linking two major roads.

HORSE TRAMWAYS: TABLE OF ROUTE OPENING DATES

Track	Constructed By	Authorised By Act Of	Inspected	Services Began
Pendleton–Albert Bridge }	Salford	1875	15-5-1877	18-5-1877
Albert Bridge–Grove Inn }	Manchester	1875	15-5-1877	18-5-1877
Grove Inn–Kersal	Salford	1875	3-7-1877	30-7-1877
Oldfield Road, Regent Road, Eccles New Road, Weaste to Ladywell *	Salford	1875	16-1-1878	17-1-1878
Eccles–Patricroft–Peel Green	Barton & Eccles	1877	27-5-1878	1-6-1878
Church Street–Gildabrook	Barton & Eccles	1877	27-5-1878	19-3-1879
Pendleton, Eccles Old Roadto Gildabrook	Salford	1875	18-3-1879	19-3-1879
Blackfriars Street and part of Chapel Street **	Salford	1875	28-2-1880	** 5-1880
Pendleton–Irlams O'Th' Height }	Salford	1875	12-5-1880	12-5-1880
Irlams O'T'Ht. to Swinton}	MC&TCo.	1879	12-5-1880	12-5-1880
Blackfriars Road, Great Clowes Street, Broughton Lane, Camp Street, Lower Broughton Road to Cliff	Salford	1875	10-9-1880	11-9-1880
Goodiers Lane–Trafford Road loop for Racecourse	Salford	1885	1-6-1886	14-6-1886
Lower Broughton Road from Broughton Bridge to Camp St.	Salford	1885	23-8-1887	8-1887
Irlams O'Th'Height to Pendlebury; Station Road	MC&TCo.	898	14-12-1898	14-12-189
Cross Lane–Trafford Road	Salford	1897		3-6-1901

Notes: The Bury New Road track was altered from single-line with passing loops to double track throughout, and was inspected and approved 24-3-18{
   Broad Street was relaid in 1888, and Regent Road in 1891. The lines along Cross Lane and Trafford Road to Trafford Bridge were never worked by t
   Carriage Company.

* The section of Regent Road between Oldfield Road and Regent Bridge was not used for traffic until December 1880.

** The outward track only was used from May 1880.

4

Preparation for Electric Traction

n the 1890s the Manchester Carriage & Tramways Company faced an uncertain future. Leases of the municipal lines in Salford and Manchester were due to expire towards the turn of the century, and there was no guarantee that they would be renewed. Indeed, Parliament's opposition to the idea of local authorities operating their own tramways had been removed by a bill introduced in 1893 by the Municipal Corporations Association. As early as October 1894, there was a motion in the Salford Highways Committee to seek powers to work the tramways. It resulted in an equal number of votes for and against the motion, but because the Chairman refused to exercise his casting vote, it was not carried. The idea did not die, however, and in February 1895 a sub-committee was set up to investigate the desirability of municipal operation of the tramways. The recommendation of that sub-committee was again not carried, for some believed that the existing method of leasing the tramways was very profitable for the Corporation, and that it would be foolish for the local authority to take on additional expenditure and responsibility. At this time the annual rental received by Salford from the Company totalled £8,852-2s-0d. It was decided to defer the matter for reconsideration, but to extend the lease of the Salford lines, due to expire in 1898, so as to be co-terminous with the Manchester leases expiring on the 27th April 1901. The two Corporations also jointly agreed that increased rentals should be charged to the Company if the leases were renewed. The Company immediately agreed to an increased rental, and offered to work the tramway system with a new form of traction, but pointed out their reluctance to incur great expense in view of the short time the leases had to run. An extension of the leases for a further ten years was requested, but refused.

The Company was left in a difficult situation. It possessed some 500 tramcars and more than 5000 horses, housed in some twenty separate depot and stabling establishments throughout the region, operated services over 143 route miles, and owned many lengths of track in the outer suburbs. The directors were understandably reluctant to make any further major investment until the future was decided. Yet experience elsewhere with other forms of motive power indicated that the horse-drawn era was coming to a close. Whether the horse would be replaced by steam, gas or electric traction was not as yet clear, but it was not the time to fall behind with developments. The Company still retained hopes of regaining powers to operate services in the whole of the region, and therefore attempted to co-operate with the municipal authorities as far as was possible. By 1896, both Salford and Manchester Corporations had determined to operate the lines themselves, and the Company itself introduced a Parliamentary bill to enable it to work the tramways by electrical power. This was opposed by most of the local authorities, and was consequently lost.

In Salford, the Corporation revived the idea of constructing lines along Cross Lane and the whole of Trafford Road, and gained authorisation to do so in 1897, though the work was not carried out until much later. The Company suggested that the Eccles New Road line to Weaste should be doubled, but the Corporation reacted by reminding the Company officials that they had previously turned down this idea. In the end, a compromise was reached, the Company agreeing to pay £300 per annum towards the cost of constructing the double track on Eccles New Road, but only 7½% rental on that and the Cross Lane section, when the latter was built. The Manchester Ship Canal construction work, followed by its opening in 1894, had brought greatly increased traffic to these roads.

The residents of Pendlebury finally obtained their tramway in 1898, after the Company had been persuaded to construct a line from the junction at Irlams O'Th'Height, along Bolton Road to the Windmill Hotel, and along Station Road to join the existing tracks at Swinton. The opening of this new line was the occasion of an interesting demonstration.

Residents of Swinton gained a tramway eighteen years earlier, but passengers for the Pendlebury area had to endure the horse-drawn omnibus until almost the end of the horse-tramway era. In 1898 the Carriage Company, anxious to be seen to oblige and hoping to secure its future as its leases of other lines expired, finally agreed to construct a tramway through Pendlebury to connect with the existing lines at Irlams O'Th'Height and at Swinton Church. The new line was mainly single-track with passing loops. In this view of Bolton Road, Pendlebury, the workmen are laying the track approaching one of the loops.
(Photo courtesy Salford Local History Library)

Finishing touches are applied to the road surface near the Windmill Hotel, Pendlebury, to complete track-laying in 1898. Although the track was relatively new, it was not deemed substantial enough for the electric tramcars which were to commence in Salford in 1901. Salford Corporation would not consider re-laying the lines until the arbitration award for their purchase by the Swinton & Pendlebury U.D.C. from the Carriage Company had been settled. When the reconstruction took place, the opportunity was taken to double the track on the Bolton Road section, although Station Road, being narrower, remained single with passing loops.
(Photo courtesy Salford Local History Library)

Company Experiments

In determining what the future form of motive power was going to be, the Company was alive to various possibilities. Construction of new horse cars at the Pendleton Works was suspended, whilst newer forms of traction were investigated. Experience on the steam tramways, such as the Manchester, Bury, Rochdale & Oldham Company's lines, had demonstrated that the use of a separate locomotive drawing a pasenger trailer was somewhat cumbersome and unwieldy, but steam tramcars of a different style were popular in Paris. In that city, cars designed by Monsieur Leon Serpollet, in which both locomotive and passenger accommodation were combined in one unit, were operating successfully. The Carriage Company arranged for a sample Serpollet car to be delivered to their Rusholme Depot, and on the 17th February 1898, the inventor himself came to Manchester to give a demonstration drive around the city. Although reports were favourable, the fact that the two large local authorities had already indicated a preference for electric traction persuaded the Company to allow its interest to lapse.

Likewise, in nearby Trafford Park, which had been purchased in 1896 for development as an industrial estate, four gas-engined tramcars owned by the British Gas Traction Company, had been working on a line from Barton to the Trafford Road entrance, and their operation had been watched with interest by Company officials. John Eades believed that the gas tramcars were too complicated and too expensive to maintain, and that their smell was objectionable. "They fail," he said, "when they have to face anything like a hill."

Meanwhile, the Corporations had recognised that electricity was to be the motive power of the future, and had set about reviewing the best method of application. At one time there was an inclination in Salford in favour of the conduit system, but when Manchester announced its preference for the overhead wire method of current collection, the advisability of adopting a similar course became obvious. This decision by the Corporations influenced the next experiment. The Company was anxious to convince both the public and the local authorities that theirs was the best qualified organisation to work the new tramways. Accordingly, at the Pendleton Works, John Eades adapted one of his patent reversible horse cars to be propelled by electricity, as if running on the overhead wire system. The car was fitted with two 15-horse-power electric motors. Being a single-ended car, it needed only one controller, Eades seeing no difficulty in adapting his reversible idea for electric tramcars. But as no part of the tramway system was as yet equipped with electrical power, he arranged for the current to be drawn from storage batteries placed under the seats. The first demonstration run took place in June 1898 for the benefit of members of the Moss Side District Council, and it was said that, although the battery arrangement was only temporary, there was sufficient power stored for the car to run up to

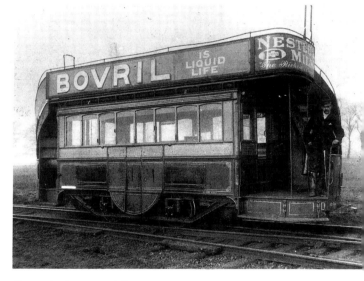

Towards the turn of the century, different forms of motive power were considered. In 1896 Trafford Park saw gas-propelled tramcars operating between the Trafford Road entrance and Barton, on a line shared with the railway goods traffic. Here, one of the cars is seen near the Barton running shed. Although the Park was to develop into a highly-concentrated industrial estate, its rural nature at this early stage is apparent.

twelve miles. At the end of a journey, freshly charged accumulators could be substituted in a few minutes. At the conclusion of this novel experiment those involved expressed themselves as highly delighted with the car's performance.

The battery car appeared again for the inaugural run over the new lines to Pendlebury on the 14th December 1898. Once again it was in charge of John Eades and his son, also John, as it left the Pendleton Works at 7.00 p.m. to collect members of the Swinton & Pendlebury Council from their offices in Victoria Park. The car's interior was lit by six incandescent lamps, two coloured at each end, and two plain near the centre, and made an interesting sight on the dark winter evening. From Victoria Park, the battery car traversed the existing tracks to Swinton, and then passed over the new line in Station Road and Bolton Road, Pendlebury, to return to the junction at

In 1898 John Eades, hoping to demonstrate the ability of the Carriage Company to work with a new form of motive power, adapted one of his patent reversible horse-cars to run on electric power. The current was drawn from storage batteries carried beneath the seats, but the vehicle was capable of taking power from an overhead wire, had any part of the system been so equipped. The car, number P 22, is standing on a line laid in to connect the Ford Lane Works with the track layout at Pendleton. John Eades stands with his hand on the controller, whilst his son, also John, is on the rear platform.

Irlams O'Th'Height. Here, the car turned on its pivot and conveyed the travellers to a celebration in the Bull's Head Hotel, Swinton. It was noted that the car then returned to the Pendleton Works in 19 minutes, but, sadly, this seems to have been the last recorded appearance of this unique vehicle. It may be that John Eades had in mind the running of battery cars during the transitional period when the tramways would have to be reconstructed and equipped for electric traction. However, it would seem that this particular tramcar was later stripped of its electrical equipment and reverted to its former condition as an ordinary horse car operating on the Pendleton route. Eades affirmed his belief in the reversible principle, and claimed that the single-ended, shorter, lighter tramcar could work equally well for electric traction. Any objection to it pivoting in the busy streets of a town centre, could be obviated by installing turning loops, or arranging services so as to terminate by going round a block of buildings, as, in fact, the horse tramcars were already doing at the Manchester end of routes. The new lines just opened offered such an opportunity, for alternate cars could diverge at the Irlams O'Th'Height junction, those to Swinton returning via Pendlebury, and vice versa, thus dispensing with the need for reversing at a terminus.

Salford's Deputation To Hamburg

As part of the policy of collecting information about the best methods of operation, the Council had sent a deputation on a three-day visit to Hamburg and its adjoining town of Altona, a region which was compared to the twin cities of Salford and Manchester. The Hamburg tramway system was at that time widely admired, and electric cars had been in use on parts of the system there since 1894. An earlier party to visit the Continent had been from Liverpool, whose councillors had arranged for a specimen car and trailer from Hamburg to be tried out in their city. As a result, the first orders for Liverpool's electric cars had been placed with a German firm, building to the Hamburg design. Salford's deputation noted that the Hamburg tramways were owned by private companies, and that the former steam and horse tramcars had been superseded over a four year period by electric tramcars, working on the overhead wire system. At the time of their visit, only a few short lengths of track in Altona were still worked by horse-drawn tramcars - operating on the guide-wheel principle as used in Salford in 1861! The members noted the cleanliness of the roads used by the electric cars in comparison with those used by the horse cars.

A report was presented to the Council in December 1898, detailing the types of tramcar seen. It recorded that single-deck cars were used throughout, hauling trailers, many of which were former horse cars. The largest type of car, 36 feet long, could accommodate 30 passengers inside and 9 standing on the platforms, but others, of the type tested in Liverpool, had seats for only 20 in the motor car and 18 in the trailer. It was noted that some 20 inches of width was allowed per passenger on the longitudonal seats, as against the more usual 16 inches in Britain. Everything was investigated, including overhead equipment, repair facilities, crew uniforms, and safety equipment, even down to the provision of 'bridge rails' carried by the Fire Brigade to enable tramcars to pass over their water hoses. The report included one section which must have pleased John Eades. The deputation had noted that in front of the Hamburg Town Hall, were the termini of several routes, "*in and out of which the cars run by reversing, necessitating changing positions of drivers and conductors, and thereby causing delay.*" Shunting operations involving the trailer cars added further complications to the city-centre arrangements, and the report commented that "*much confusion arose in busy times from the use of reversing terminal lines.*" However, the deputation also noted intended changes : "*All these termini are to be altered into circuits around the square, and also circuits around adjoining blocks of buildings, so that the cars may run continuously and without any delay and danger from reversing.*"

Amongst assorted comments about the working practices of the Hamburg tramways, the report recorded, "*A green tablet is hung on the rear end of each car for the odd purpose of indicating the direction it is NOT going.*" The deputation praised the value of first-class car construction, heavy and rigid tramrails, and artistic metalwork in posts, brackets, and 'rosettes' fixed to buildings for supporting overhead wires, "*as compared with the shapeless and absolutely ugly structures used on some of the earlier electric tramways.*" It commended the excellence of the Hamburg system, and appended a translation of the town's tramway regulations.

John Eades, who had been engaged in the manufacture of rolling stock for 36 years, and Manager of the Company's Pendleton Works for the past 32 years, was sought out by an enterprising journalist as one eminently qualified to comment on the Hamburg report. He was reported as saying that there were three types of tramcar to choose from - the Hamburg-type single-deck with trailer; the type used in Leeds and Bristol; and his own design. He thought that the Hamburg system was not suitable for Manchester and Salford, as the cars were expensive and heavy for the number of passengers they could carry. The Leeds and Bristol cars had platforms which were too long, frames which were too heavy, and fixed wheelbases which caused problems on tight curves, but they could carry passengers on the top deck, and experience in Glasgow had demonstrated that the public preferred double-deck cars. But his own reversible design was neater, lighter, and more comfortable for passengers; the small platform in front offered a good view for the driver and a large canopy protected him from the weather; the outside seats, being stationary, needed no reversible back-rests. The only possible objection was to the pivotting procedure, which could be obviated easily by the proper arrangement of route termini.

John Eades, Senior, 1841-1916. Entering the service of John Greenwood, Junior, in 1862 as a coach-maker, from 1867 Eades was Manager of the Carriage Company's Pendleton Works, where many hundreds of horse-trams were constructed and repaired under his supervision. In 1899 he built there a sample electric tramcar for Manchester, but as municipal authorities took over the running of their own transport services, the Company's empire dwindled and within a short time the Works had closed. *(Photo courtesy R. Eades.)*

Eades added that he was sorry to see a town like Liverpool placing orders for Hamburg-type cars abroad, for tramcars could be built just as well at home, and he hoped that Manchester and Salford would not fall into this error. Experience in Liverpool was to prove him correct, for that town was attempting to dispose of its German-built cars as early as 1901.

The Municipal Decision

The long-awaited but inevitable decision to assume municipal operation of the tramways, and to convert them for electric traction, was taken in 1899, when Salford promoted a Parliamentary Bill for that purpose. Having gained such powers, notice was given to the Company that the Corporation would assume full responsibility for the tramway services after the 27th April 1901 on the expiration of the lease. Manchester Corporation having reached a similar decision, a long period of uncertainty was ended for the Company. No fewer than fifteen separate local authorities were embraced by the Company's system, each of which could, in theory, have chosen to work its own district tramways. In fact, Salford, Ashton, Oldham, Stockport and Manchester having announced their intention to operate independently, the various authorities sorted themselves out into four main camps, despite Manchester entertaining ambitions to be the dominant authority

throughout the region. There was some competition for the favours of the smaller authorities. Eccles, cut off from the proposed Manchester system by the Borough of Salford, was canvassed by two separate electrical syndicates (one of which became the South Lancashire Tramways Company), both wishing to construct tramways to connect Eccles with Worsley, Farnworth, Radcliffe, Prestwich and Whitefield. Eventually, Eccles entered into an agreement with Salford for the working of the lines in its area, as also did Swinton. The Kearsley Urban District Council asked Salford whether the tramways from Swinton would continue through its area, but a decision on this point was deferred. All authorities in the region agreed to adopt the same gauge of track and method of current collection, so that, in theory, inter-running arrangements between the various undertakings would present no difficulty.

In the case of Salford, as the Corporation owned all the tracks within its boundaries, it left only a straightforward problem of negotiating a mutually acceptable price for such of the tramcars, horses, accessories, and depot premises, as to enable the horse tram services in Salford, Eccles and Swinton to continue until the arrangements for electrical operation were complete. Eccles, too, owned its own tramway tracks, but the Swinton and Pendlebury lines were Company-built, and eventually arbitration proceedings had to decide the price which the Swinton Council had to pay the Company to purchase the lines in its area.

In contrast to the Salford proposal, Manchester arranged a gradual take-over, the Company agreeing to continue operating the horse tram services until each separate route was ready for electric traction. There, too, long drawn-out arbitration proceedings had to decide a purchase price, which was complicated by the extension of the Manchester boundaries to include several stretches of Company-owned track.

Both Salford and Manchester made arrangements with the Company which would enable the reconstruction of the tracks for electric traction to commence before the expiration of the lease, and developments were pursued with vigour during 1899.

The Eades Sample Electric Car, 1899

The 1898 battery car did not end Eades' experimental work, for in the following year, when Manchester Corporation invited tenders for the supply of sample electric tramcars, he asked permission to build such a car at the Pendleton Works. His son, John Eades, junior, had been appointed to be Manchester's first Car Works Manager in March 1899, and his father's sample electric car was ready for his Committee's inspection in August of that year. In deference to the Committee's specifications, it was a double-ended, double-deck open-top tramcar, designed to seat 43 passengers, fitted with a Brill 21E truck, and electrical equipment from the Walker Company, supplied by the Dick, Kerr Company of Preston. Of the six sample cars submitted, the Pendleton-built specimen was judged to be excellently finished, and the Committee noted that great care had been exercised in its construction. It was agreed that it should be purchased for £600, and it duly entered the Manchester fleet as number 101, the lowest number carried by any Manchester Corporation electric tramcar. The Manchester Committee decided not to adopt in its entirety any one of the types inspected, but to try to combine the best features of each. However, orders were not placed with the Carriage & Tramways Company, because it was felt that the Pendleton Works had not the capacity to produce the number of tramcars required in such a short time.

Understandings With Manchester

Preliminary discussions between the two main authorities led to a number of mutually-agreed points of policy. It was proposed, for example, that tramcars should not wait or turn round in the city centre streets, and that every tramcar passing from Salford over one of the Irwell bridges would enter Manchester by one route and leave by another. Salford also felt it necessary to have a place where cars could wait for a few minutes to keep to their accurate time, and which would be a starting point for extra journeys, as, for example, during meetings at the Racecourse. To this end, there was an attempt in 1899 to acquire by compulsory purchase the land alongside Victoria Bridge Street in order to create a tramway terminus. The London & North Western Railway Company had bought this land some years earlier, on the opening of Exchange Station in 1884, but had not used it. The Salford Council argued that as the land was at a lower level, it could not be used for railway purposes, but the L.N.W.R. claimed it was needed for extensions to the Exchange Station offices, and the attempt to purchase failed. (In fact, the land was never used as such, but not until 1935 was it

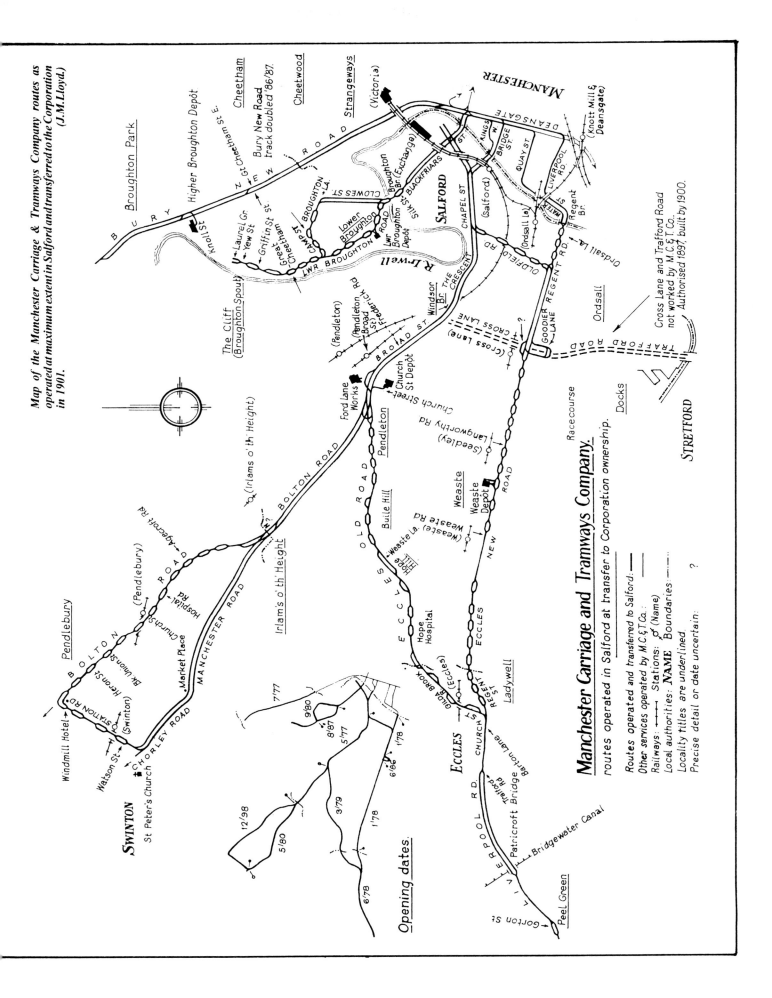

Map of the Manchester Carriage & Tramways Company routes as operated at maximum extent in Salford and transferred to the Corporation in 1901. (J.M.Lloyd.)

Manchester Carriage and Tramways Company.

routes operated in Salford at transfer to Corporation ownership.

Routes operated and transferred to Salford: ——
Other services operated by M.C.&T.Co.: ——
Railways: ⊙ (Name)
Local authorities: **NAME** Boundaries: ————
Locality titles are underlined.
Precise detail or date uncertain: ?

Opening dates.

The 1898 line along Station Road was the last new horse-drawn tramway to open in the district. Tramcar P 14 (from the Pendleton, Church Street, depot) stands on the corner at the Swinton end of Station Road, having arrived from Pendlebury. With the opening of this line, tramcars to Swinton returned to the Irlams O'Th'Height junction via Pendlebury, and vice versa. **(Photo E. Yates.)**

purchased from the then L.M.S. Railway Company for conversion into Victoria Bus Station, opened in 1937.)

Another agreement was that Manchester would have exclusive rights to work the Bury New Road routes, so Salford's negotiations with the Carriage & Tramways Company included arrangements to lease the depots at Pendleton (Church Street), Weaste, and Lower Broughton, but excluded the Higher Broughton depot at Knoll Street, which would not be required. Both Councils agreed to employ as many of the Company's workers as possible.

The two Corporations were also at one in their choice of the standard track gauge, method of current collection from overhead wires, and rules governing running into each other's territory. But the understandings were soon to become misunderstandings.

The Boer War

The war in South Africa had no influence on the impending reconstruction of the tramways, but produced yet another annoyance for the beleaguered Carriage Company, for in November 1899, Government Inspectors visited the stables at Broughton, Pendleton and Weaste, and requisitioned sixty of the best horses for the use of cavalry soldiers in the Transvaal. A number of the Company's men were used to drive the chosen animals to London Road Station, Manchester, en route to a training camp.

Orders For Electric Tramcars

In the autumn of 1899 the Council considered the results of their advertise-ment inviting tenders for the supply of 100 double-deck double-ended electric tramcars. It had been decided not to attempt to operate trailer cars. Twelve firms had submitted tenders, including Brown, Marshall & Company, of Birmingham, and Laing, Wharton & Down, of London, both of which firms failed to provide proper drawings and omitted any information about the provision of the electrical equipment. Other companies had tendered to supply cars at prices varying from £498 to £549 each, most offering delivery of all 100 cars in about 18 months. After debate and inspection, two companies supplying tramcar bodies had been selected for further consideration. The sub-committee had been impressed with the Dick Kerr production at Preston, but had liked even better the cars the Birkenhead firm of G.F.Milnes was building for Edinburgh.

Many transport undertakings were in process of converting to electric traction at about the same time, and all makers were reported to have full order books. It was imperative that decisions should be made quickly if the new cars were to be delivered within a reasonable time. The councillors were also reminded that most tramcar building firms, in order to reduce congestion in their works, stipulated that the assembly of the cars should be done in Salford. Work on the erection of the new tramcar sheds on land acquired for that purpose at the junction of Frederick Road and Seaford Road, should therefore begin immediately. A second shed on land selected at Weaste was contemplated.

There was considerable discussion about the use of local labour. It was argued that the Corporation should take advantage of local expertise, and speakers claimed that the horse cars produced at the Pendleton Works were the best in the country. The large staff of five to six hundred men would not be put out of employment if the cars were built in Salford, it was said, but

Alderman Linsley, Chairman of the Tramways Committee, reported that although John Eades had said previously that he could undertake the work, he had since sent word that he could not carry out that promise. The Carriage Company had been building some thirty new horse cars annually, but had now ceased production.

Representatives from the Tramways Committee made visits to inspect the tramway systems at Liverpool and Sheffield, and, eventually, in October 1899, a contract was awarded to the Westinghouse in nearby Trafford Park, for the supply of the electrical equipment and the Brill trucks, the car bodies to be sub-contracted to G.F.Milnes. The cost per car was to be £534 10s. 0d. The G.F.Milnes Company was a successor to the Starbuck firm which had supplied the first horse-drawn tramcars to Salford in 1877. That Company had been wound up in 1886, but its former Secretary, George F. Milnes, had purchased the factory and goodwill, and had begun to make 'garden seat' horse cars and trailers for steam tramways. By 1898 Milnes had begun to supply electric tramcars, and because the capacity of the Birkenhead works was limited, and in anticipation of the expected boom in orders for new vehicles, he purchased a more spacious site for a new factory at Hadley, in Shropshire, the Birkenhead premises becoming merely a finishing shop. There was some debate in the Council on the merits of top-covered, as against open-top cars, but it was thought that roofs would "interfere with the trolley arm and be awkward."

Alderman Linsley announced the appointment of Mr. Ernest Hatton as the first Tramway Engineer, at a salary of £240 per annum, as from the 1st December 1899. It was reported that Mr. Hatton had had much experience in the construction of tramway track, and that he was at present engaged at Birkenhead. Ernest Hatton, born 16th August 1875 at Hatton's Farm, Dallam, Burtonwood, Warrington, was but twenty-four years old at the time of his appointment. He had served an apprenticeship with the Pearson & Knowles Coal and Iron Company, before being employed in laying the tramways in Liverpool, and afterwards on the other side of the Mersey. At the time of his move to Salford, the Tramways Engineer (later designated the General Manager) was appointed for a term of twelve months only, the post being subject to review and possible re-appointment at the end of that period.

Electricity Supply, Track, And Equipment

Salford already had an electric lighting department, so it was proposed that that department should be enlarged to supply current to the tramways from a new generating station on Frederick Road, which was designed to have the capacity for all the light and power needed by the Corporation. The electricity department was told that the likely future demand for power for the tramways would be for 150 cars in use each day, with extras on Race days.

Initial orders were placed with the Leeds Steel Company for the supply of some 5000 tons of rails, to be delivered in monthly instalments, and with Russell's of Wednesbury for 500 ornamental poles to support the overhead wires, 60 to be delivered immediately, so that the work of reconstructing the tramways for electric traction could begin as soon as possible. The task of laying the new electrically-bonded rails was begun on the 24th April 1900 by the Corporation's own staff, supervised by the Tramways Engineer, Ernest Hatton. The first roads chosen for the new tramway work were Cross Lane and Trafford Road, powers for which had been gained by the Corporation in 1897. The workforce was thus able to gain experience of laying the new track on roads not used by the existing horse tram routes of the Company. The practice was to lay a six inch depth of concrete, extending to the customary eighteen inches either side of the tracks, and use this as a foundation on which to place the rails. The top surface road setts were replaced flush with the rail top once the lines had been fixed to the correct gauge. Special pieces of trackwork for junctions, etc., were first prepared and laid out for checking in the permanent way yard in Frederick Road, before being installed on site.

The clause in the 1870 Tramways Act making the tramway undertaking responsible for paving and maintaining the roadway between the track gauge and for eighteen inches on either side, had been designed originally to compensate local authorities for wear occasioned by the horses' hooves, but this was never repealed in the days of electric traction, even though the new tramcars made no use of the granite setts. Consequently, tramway managers were obliged to expend energy and resources in the upkeep of vast areas of roadway for the benefit of others, including, ultimately, their competitors.

A small official ceremony, attended by the Mayor of Salford, Alderman Rudman, centred round the erection of the first ornamental tramway

Salford Corporation acquired land on Frederick Road for the erection of a new depot to house the electric tramcar fleet. Because of pressure on pace in their works, some manufacturers of tramcar bodies insisted that final assembly of the complete cars should take place in the customer's own premises, so it was important that the buildings should be ready in good time. The shell of the Frederick Road Depot is here under construction in 1900, though no tracks have as yet been laid.

standard at the Regent Road end of Cross Lane. It had been decided that wherever the width of the roadway was sufficient, centre poles would be used to hold up the electric wiring, with side poles and span-wire construction on narrower thoroughfares. Reconstruction work on roads with existing tramways was to make use of temporary track where necessary to enable the Company's horse trams to pass any obstructions. The firm of George Hill & Company, of Trafford Electric Works, Manchester was awarded the contract for the erection of the overhead wires, a task which was carried out without any interference to the horse car services.

It was agreed that the further construction, or reconstruction, of track ready for the new electric services would proceed in the following order :-

1. New track in Frederick Road, from Broad Street to Lower Broughton Road, which would give access to the proposed new car shed at the corner of Seaford Road.

2. Reconstruction of the Pendleton route from the Woolpack Inn, via Broad Street, The Crescent, and Chapel Street to Victoria and Blackfriars Bridges to connect with Manchester lines.

3. Reconstruction of Regent Road to Regent Bridge to connect with the Manchester lines from Water Street, together with Oldfield Road to the junction with Chapel Street.

4. Reconstruction of the Lower Broughton route, along Lower Broughton Road from Broughton Bridge to Camp Street ; and along Sussex Street, Great Clowes Street, and Blackfriars Road to the junction with Chapel Street.

5. Reconstruction of Camp Street and Broughton Lane from the Lower Broughton Road junction, along Great Clowes Street to Sussex Street.

6. New track along Great Clowes Street from its junction with Broughton Lane to the junction with Bury New Road via The Cliff, there to make a junction with the Higher Broughton route.

7. Reconstruction of the Higher Broughton route on the Salford portion of Bury New Road, from the Manchester boundary at Grove Inn to the Prestwich boundary at Kersal.

8. Reconstruction of the portion of Lower Broughton Road from Camp Street to Cromwell Bridge only. (It had been decided to abandon the length of horse tramway which extended further along Lower Broughton Road beyond Great Cheetham Street.)

9. New track in New Bailey Street, from Chapel Street to the centre of Albert Bridge.

10. Reconstruction of the Eccles New Road route to Eccles from Cross Lane to the Eccles boundary at Ladywell.

11. Reconstruction of the Swinton route from Pendleton along Bolton Road to the Swinton boundary.

12. Reconstruction of the Eccles Old Road route from Pendleton to the Eccles boundary at Gilda Brook.

Agreements were entered into with the adjacent authorities of Eccles and Swinton for the reconstruction and operation of the tramways in their districts. The arrangement was that Salford would undertake the work and meet the cost of reconstruction, and thereafter would maintain the tramways in a proper state of repair. At the end of 21 years, the tramways would be handed over free of charge to the district councils. This apparently generous scheme was not without its critics from the smaller authorities, whose representatives made constant attempts to gain additional improvements (in the way of road widening, flagging, and the reconstruction of pavements and kerbs - all tasks for which they themselves should have been responsible) at the cost of the tramway operator.

By the end of October 1900 it was reported that some 7 miles of new track had been constructed, which included the Cross Lane, Trafford Road, and Frederick Road lengths, together with some on Great Clowes Street. About 400 men were employed daily to carry out this task. By February 1901 about half of the existing lines had been relaid, the horse trams continuing to run, but on the new tracks. It was stated that there had been no inconvenience to the travelling public, and practically no accidents, even though on the Pendleton route some temporary track had had to be used. The temporary track was laid in short lengths on the road surface by the side of the excavations for the new construction, and was moved onwards every alternate night after the passage of the last service car.

Arrangements With The Carriage Company

Arrangements had been made with the Carriage Company for the staff of the Pendleton Works to carry out all repairs which might be required on the horse tramcars during the period of their operation by the Corporation. The authority agreed to pay the full cost of materials and labour for such work, "plus 25% to cover establishment charges and profit." The Company, however, would still be the owner of those horse-drawn tramcars used in Manchester until all that city's lines were converted to electric traction, so in return the Company agreed that after the expiration of its lease of the Salford tracks it would "pay the sum of 1s.3d. per car each way for all cars taken over the Salford lines from Manchester to the Company's repairing shop at Pendleton, it being understood that such cars shall not carry passengers nor interfere in any way with the traffic on the tramways."

The purchase or leasing of such of the Company's property as would be necessary to continue the horse car services in Salford after the 27th April 1901, resulted in the Corporation agreeing to rent certain premises for at least two years, but the term of the lease was not to extend more than five years, namely :-

Pendleton (Church Street) Depot, for all the cars and horses required to work the Pendleton, Eccles Old Road, and Swinton routes, at a rent of £1,000.

Horse-tram services were maintained whilst preparations for the advent of electric traction went ahead. In this scene at Pendleton, a Swinton-bound horse-tram is running on temporary tracks whilst workmen construct the new lines in the centre of the roadway. The building on the extreme left is the Ford Lane Works of the Carriage Company, where the horse-tram would have been built

Weaste Depot, for the Weaste and Eccles New Road routes, at £630.

Lower Broughton Depot, for the Lower Broughton routes, at £250.

Pendleton Offices (£120) and Grain Stores (£250).

The Higher Broughton Depot at Knoll Street was not included, as it was intended that Manchester Corporation should work the Bury New Road routes when converted for electric traction, and the Company was to maintain its existing horse-tram services to Kersal in the meantime. Likewise, the main portion of the Pendleton Works was not required by the Corporation, but was to continue in use by the Company for the repair and maintenance of vehicles.

The Corporation also agreed to purchase outright 900 horses and 94 tramcars on terms settled by valuers at £42,000. Mr.C.R.Bellamy, General Manager of the Liverpool tramways, was invited to act as valuer on behalf of the Salford Corporation at a fee of twelve guineas per day. Items to be purchased comprised the contents of the three depots to be leased, as under:-

Pendleton: 400 horses and 38 double-deck tramcars, of which 20 were for the Pendleton route, 14 for Swinton, and 4 for the Eccles Old Road route to Patricroft.

Weaste: 400 horses and 37 double-deck tramcars, of which 33 were for the Weaste route and 4 for the Eccles New Road route to Peel Green.

Lower Broughton: 100 horses, 16 single-deck (one-horse) tram-cars, and 3 double-deck tramcars for the Lower Broughton routes to The Cliff, and short-workings thereof as far as Sussex Street or Broughton Lane.

It will be noted that for each double-deck two-horse tramcar, a stud of some ten horses had to be maintained. The tramcars were listed according to their allocation, because under Company operation interchangeability was re-stricted by virtue of the fact that route details were painted on the sides of the majority of vehicles, thereby limiting their use to one particular service. The small number of tramcars listed for the long routes to Patricroft and Peel Green reflected the half-hourly frequency of those services, whereas the greater number allocated to the inner-city sections of routes indicated the higher frequency, and included extra cars for short-workings in busy periods. By this date, the service to Swinton had been increased to a 15 minute frequency, with cars as far as Pendleton every five minutes. Similarly, extra cars on the Weaste route provided a five-minute frequency as far as Cross Lane junction. The small one-horse single-deck cars from the Lower Broughton Depot were used on the Sussex Street to Deansgate service, which boasted a two-minute frequency during busy periods, four minutes during the rest of the day, and two-and-a-half minutes all day on Saturdays, whilst the full route to The Cliff operated only half-hourly. After the 27th April 1901, on the expiration of the Company's lease, the Corporation intended to assume responsibility for maintaining all the existing horse-tram services, whilst preparing for the advent of electric traction. It was hoped that the first electric tramcars would be running by October 1901.

In the meantime, Ernest Hatton was planning some radical changes to the Company system of operating the horse trams. Instead of each route terminating in Manchester, he proposed that under muncipal control, services which ran to Deansgate or Victoria from opposite sides of the city would be linked, so that longer through routes would be offered, and passengers would not need to change cars. His scheme would have linked Weaste and Lower Broughton; Peel Green and Broughton; Swinton and Broughton (Great Clowes Street), all via Manchester, and would have provided improved frequencies on the inner parts of popular services, such as from Pendleton to Manchester. In addition, he planned to introduce a new Circular Route running from Blackfriars Street, via Chapel Street, Broad Street, Frederick Road, Great Clowes Street, and back to Blackfriars. This latter route would not have crossed Manchester's boundary, but would have remained solely on Salford lines. He estimated that 130 horse-trams would be needed to institute the proposed improved services, 36 more than the number agreed to be purchased from the Carriage Company. Although additional horses were readily available, extra tramcars were not so easily acquired, but as they would be required for only a short time until the conversion of the first routes to electric operation released vehicles for use on other parts of the system, it was deemed unnecessary to purchase

additional cars for temporary use. As it happened, however, the difficulties presented by the dispute over inter-running with Manchester combined to defeat Ernest Hatton's ambitious plans.

Tramway Workers' Wages And Hours Of Work

At the turn of the century the wage earned by the driver or conductor of a horse-tram varied from three-shillings-and-eightpence to four-shillings-and-sixpence per day, according to the number of hours worked. The weekly total reached an average of £1.4s.0d. for a six-day working week of about 10½ hours per day. Working rotas were based on a three-weekly cycle :

1st Week : 6 days at 10½ hours	=	63 hours.
2nd Week : 6 days at 10½ hours,		
plus 8½ hours on Sunday	=	71½ hours.
3rd Week : 6 days at 10½ hours,		
plus 13½ hours on Sunday	=	76½ hours.
Total for three weeks	=	211 hours.

In pursuance of the stated policy of offering employment to as many of the Carriage Company workers as possible, and in order to maintain the existing horse-tram services during the reconstruction period, members of the Tramways Committee visited the horse-tram depots to meet staff and to invite the respective managers to continue in that capacity after the take-over. At Weaste, depot manager C.H.Chester agreed, but at Pendleton, Robert Guest, a long-serving Company employee with over 53 years' service dating from the Greenwood era, said he intended to retire.His deputy, F.T.South, agreed to continue, but wanted an increase in salary. At Lower Broughton, G.P.Jones agreed to continue on his existing salary. The Tramways Committee also resolved that "*the four men who are at present engaged by the Manchester Carriage & Tramways Company in the starting of cars at Deansgate, Pendleton, and Regent Road be engaged for similar work.*" In the case of the Deansgate man, however, as he would not be employed solely for the benefit of cars on the Salford routes, it was agreed that the Company should be asked to pay a portion of his wages. The employees referred to supervised the loading and departure of cars at particularly busy junctions. At the same meeting it was agreed that the parcels traffic on the tramcars would not be continued in Salford.

The Disagreement With Manchester

Unhappily, although heads of agreement to cover running in each other's territory had been drawn up by the respective Tramways Committees, a dispute arose over the interpretation of clauses which appeared to give Manchester the right to dictate the pattern of the Salford services. It was argued that Manchester would have the power to impose the route, the frequency, and the numbers of Salford cars using their lines to Deansgate, so as to gain the maximum possible revenue from the traffic receipts. The Salford Council insisted that the "*Salford Corporation shall be entitled to make the fullest possible use of the Salford lines.*" A payment per car mile had been agreed for vehicles using Manchester tracks, but Salford wished to retain the authority to organise its own routes and services. Whilst the arguments raged, a temporary arrangement was reached, whereby for two months from the 27th April 1901 Salford agreed to pay to Manchester a sum equal to the Carriage Company's track rental per mile, plus 3.57 pence per car mile run, for the use of the lines within the Manchester boundary from the bridges over the River Irwell to Deansgate. This also gave Salford the right to run the horse trams round the Victoria Buildings to avoid turning them in the centre of the roadway, which right was to "absolutely cease" as soon as the electric cars came into use.

The Salford Town Clerk offered Manchester the opportunity to operate the route to Kersal by horse traction for two months, on the same terms as demanded from Salford for working Manchester lines to Deansgate, but as it was intended that the Carriage Company would continue to operate this service until Manchester had completed the conversion work, the offer did not carry great force, and remained unanswered.

An additional worry for Salford was that, although Manchester had agreed to Salford vehicles joining Bury New Road via Great Clowes Street at Bella Vista to travel as far as the Prestwich boundary at Kersal, the larger city had also claimed the exclusive right to build and work the direct route to the city centre. It was felt that this concession would jeopardise the success of projected Salford lines along Great Cheetham Street and what later became the Leicester Road route to Bury Old Road, and consequently, although prepared to consider joint working, it was resolved that under no circumstances could they envisage another Corporation owning and operating a tramway in Salford's own territory. Prestwich and Whitefield were to remain at liberty to enter into agreements for the leasing or working of their lines either with Manchester or Salford, but, clearly, might be influenced in their choice by the operator providing the most direct route into Manchester.

It was hoped that suitable arrangements between the two authorities would have been settled before the commencement of the first electric tramcar services began.

Salford's Purchase Of The Horse Tramway

The transfer to municipal operation of the existing horse tramcar routes in Salford, intended to take place on Sunday the 28th April 1901, suffered an unexpected eleventh-hour set-back when a misunderstanding arose over the valuation of the Carriage Company's property which was to be transferred. There appeared to be a difference of £5000 between the sum offered by Salford and the amount expected by the Company. Neither side would give way, and it seemed likely that there would be no tramcar services operating in the Salford area from the 29th April. Company representatives were in London attending the hearing of the Manchester Corporation Bill, and a hurried journey to the capital by Salford officials resulted in a temporary arrangement being agreed, whereby the Company continued to work the services for two extra days only, on the Monday and Tuesday. At first, there appeared to be no prospect of an early settlement. The Company's lease of the Salford lines had now expired, and would not be renewed. It did not seem possible for the Corporation to obtain horses and tramcars elsewhere at such short notice. Late on the Tuesday evening, Alderman Henry Linsley, Chairman of the Salford Tramways Committee, made a desperate attempt to ensure the continuation of the services on the following day. He made a midnight visit to Sir John Harwood, the Company

Alderman Henry Linsley, Chairman of the Salford Tramways Committee from 1898 to 1921, guided the undertaking through the early years of municipal ownership.

Chairman, during the course of which it emerged that a telegram sent by the Company from London had not been received by the Salford Tramways Committee. This telegram had contained an offer to divide the amount under dispute. On learning of this new development, and subject to the full Council's approval on the following day, Alderman Linsley immediately agreed to the purchase of the cars, horses and equipment at the new price of £42,500, and Sir John Harwood gave an undertaking that the cars would run as normal. The money was paid to the Company on the afternoon of Wednesday, the 1st May 1901, and on the following day Salford Corporation became the owner of 906 horses and 94 tramcars.

The General Manager's forecast for the period ending in March 1902 was that he would operate for six months with the full complement of 94 horse-trams, then, as electric car routes opened, that total would be reduced to 84 for five months, some to be used on new routes which would be inaugurated as track was completed. At this stage, the intention was that the Pendleton and Cross Lane routes would be the first to be converted to operation by electric tramcars.

The first tramcar service actually operated by the Salford authority left the Pendleton office at 4.30 a.m. on the Thursday morning, the 2nd May 1901. General Manager Ernest Hatton was present and noted that the first journey brought receipts of eight shillings and twopence. The Corporation had undertaken to offer employment to as many of the Carriage Company workers as possible, and the existing horse tram services were maintained, so the transfer would have passed largely unnoticed by the travelling public had it not been for the introduction of Bell Punch tickets to replace the old fare collection boxes. This innovation did not please some passengers, who felt that if they had to be issued with a ticket, and retain it for possible inspection, they were not being trusted. Letters to the local press denounced the punches and tickets as "badges of servitude," "useless," "insulting," and claimed that the new methods would "reduce pasengers to the level of the herd." However, it was clear that the issue of tickets would greatly assist accounting procedures, as well as providing proof that each passenger had paid a fare, and it was announced that Manchester intended to adopt the same system when their electric tramcar services began.

In anticipation of the difficulties with Manchester, Ernest Hatton had been authorised to construct tracks in the lower end of Chapel Street, leading to Victoria Bridge Street, from which to work the traffic whilst the Blackfriars Street lines were under reconstruction. Within a month he was able to institute a new horse tram route. On Monday, the 3rd June 1901 he inaugurated a new service from Victoria Bridge to the Docks, via Oldfield Road and Regent Road, and using the newly-laid lines in Trafford Road as far as the swing bridge over the Manchester Ship Canal at the Salford boundary with Stretford. The new route was operated by six horse-trams, offering a 10 minute frequency, at fares of one penny from Victoria to Cross Lane, and a further penny from Cross Lane to Trafford Bridge. At the same time, the new service encountered some minor competition from the Trafford Park Estates Company, which had begun an omnibus service from Pendleton to Old Trafford (at a penny fare) to connect with their gas tram service at the Trafford Park entrance on the Stretford side of Trafford Bridge.

On Thursday the 27th June, the two-month temporary agreement for the use of Manchester's tracks to Deansgate expired, and with no sign of an immediate settlement of the dispute, the Salford horse trams ceased running over the River Irwell bridges, the river being the dividing line between Manchester and Salford. From the following day, all services were altered so as to terminate at the borough boundary on Blackfriars Bridge, the nearest possible point to Manchester's business centre. Men working on the construction of the new electric lines elsewhere in the city were moved to reconstruct the terminal lines at the junction of Blackfriars Street and Chapel Street, and after the last car had left Blackfriars Bridge on the Saturday evening, a large staff of men began the work of widening the roadway. The setting back of the pavements was necessary to avoid accident, as when the reversible Eades cars were turning, their platforms overlapped the footpaths. Crossovers were laid so as to use both lines on the bridge as terminal stubs, though cars were unable to turn when another car was on the adjoining track. As the differences seemed unlikely to be resolved, some Salford councillors urged the Corporation to buy a piece of vacant land which lay on Blackfriars Street between the River Irwell and Chapel Street, in order to have space available for a main terminus.

The lines over the Irwell bridges on Regent Road, New Bailey Street, and Victoria Bridge Street remained unused. As a result, Manchester, whose first electric tramcar service from Albert Square to Cheetham Hill had begun on the 6th June, felt obliged to purchase 11 horse trams and 142 horses in order to provide a temporary service from its side of Regent Bridge

Failure to reach agreement with Manchester over running rights to Deansgate meant that the Salford services terminated at the boundary on Blackfriars Bridge, where alterations to the track layout allowed two terminal stubs to be used to the very centre of the bridge. However, reversing the cars proved hazardous, as their bodies overhung the pavement when turning. No doubt the police constables seen on the right of the picture were on duty to supervise these operations. A car for Higher Broughton (B17) receives passengers as a Cross Lane car arrives via the facing points. Notice the lady with the large hat - a warning was issued about the possible danger to other passengers from long hat-pins, and ladies were requested to exercise care in their use.

(Photo A.Astle.)

o Deansgate and St.Mary's Gate. This service was to complete the link between its boundaries at Regent Bridge and at the Grove Inn on Bury New Road, to which point Manchester had commenced to run a new electric car route on the same date that Salford horse cars had begun to terminate at Blackfriars Bridge. Manchester passengers travelling from Regent Bridge to the Grove Inn thus had to change from horse to electric car at St.Mary's Gate, just a few yards away from the Salford terminus. Just as the Salford vehicles were barred from using the Manchester lines across the municipal boundary, so the Manchester trams were denied use of the higher reaches of Bury New Road, which later would have given access to Prestwich, Whitefield and Bury.
Residents of Higher Broughton were likewise denied their direct route into Manchester, unless they were prepared to change vehicles at the boundary. Ernest Hatton had to make arrangements to offer an alternative to the former Company route, and therefore instituted one more service than he had originally planned. He was able to re-schedule the inner portion of the former route from Kersal so as to use only Salford tracks, and the new service commenced towards the end of June 1901, leaving Blackfriars Bridge by way of Blackfriars Road and Great Clowes Street. A foretaste of

difficulties to recur some 25 years later was presented by the problem of subsidence at The Cliff near the top of Great Clowes Street, which temporarily prevented the running of cars at that point, so outward-bound cars used part of Great Cheetham Street before joining Bury New Road for the last stage of the journey to Kersal. However, on the inward journey, Hatton had arranged for the horse trams to continue along Bury New Road past its junction with Great Cheetham Street, to the nearest possible point to the Manchester boundary. Here, Upper Camp Street, a minor thoroughfare on the western side of Bury New Road leading to Great Clowes Street, was equipped with temporary single-track to enable the horse trams to rejoin their outward route as near the city centre as possible, an attempt, no doubt, to capture some of the passengers who might otherwise have joined the Manchester cars at the Grove Inn.
Ernest Hatton had taken the opportunity to purchase 106 extra horses, only 55 of which were intended for the Higher Broughton route. Of the others, 11 were for Lower Broughton, and 40 for extra routes which he hoped to open before the advent of the electric cars. It was reported that the whole of three depots were working to their full extent, that receipts were satisfactory, but that additional tramcars would have been an advantage.

Double-deck horse-trams from other depots had to be redeployed to serve on the Higher Broughton route. Passengers made known their dissatisfaction with the congestion and crowding on Blackfriars Bridge, and hoped for an early end to the dispute.

Consequently, some alteration of the arrangements at the Manchester end of the routes took place, and by August 1901 the services were advertised as follows :-

From BLACKFRIARS BRIDGE to :
    HIGHER BROUGHTON (KERSAL) every 5 minutes.
    TRAFFORD BRIDGE every 10 minutes.
    CROSS LANE every few minutes.
    WEASTE every 5 minutes.
    PENDLETON every few minutes.

From VICTORIA BRIDGE to:
    SWINTON every 30 minutes.
    PENDLEBURY every 30 minutes.
    PATRICROFT (via ECCLES OLD ROAD) 30 minutes.
    PEEL GREEN (via ECCLES NEW ROAD) 30 minutes.
    WALNESS (FREDERICK) ROAD every few minutes.
    CLIFF (LOWER BROUGHTON) every 15 minutes.

When Salford assumed operation of the horse-tram services, the fare collection boxes were withdrawn and tickets were issued for the first time. The young guard is provided with cash bag and ticket punch, although the occasion appears to be a Sunday School outing. Horse-trams were re-allocated to other parts of the city as electric services developed, and in this case a Weaste car, W 27, is seen on Lower Broughton Road at its junction with Walness Road (the old name for Frederick Road), a district which it would not normally have served.

5

The Opening of the
First Electric Tramway Routes

The horse trams operating from Blackfriars and Victoria Bridges during the summer of 1901 continued to provide the basic services whilst preparations continued for the advent of the electric tramcars. It was reported that a permanent supply of electric current would not be available for some two months, but early in August a battery sub-station at Strawberry Hill (Frederick Road) was able to provide temporary motive power to a limited area for driver-training purposes, and overhead equipment in Frederick Road and Seaford Road, alongside the new depot premises, had been completed with that intention. General Manager Ernest Hatton's connections with Liverpool proved useful, when two men from that undertaking were engaged to train Salford men as crew for the new electric tramcars. Hatton's original idea had been to send the men to Liverpool for such training, but C.R.Bellamy had replied that Liverpool streets were so congested, it would be better for the driving instruction to take place in Salford.

At this time it was optimistically announced that twenty of the new tramcars were ready for immediate delivery, but as many transport undertakings in the British Isles had placed orders for vehicles at about the same time, the few existing suppliers were finding difficulty in keeping all customers satisfied. Originally, Westinghouse and Milnes had undertaken to supply twelve complete tramcars by November 1900, and it would appear that the Trafford Park firm had, indeed, been as good as its word, for in January 1901 the Westinghouse asked for 50% payment for the trucks and electrical equipment then in store at one of the Manchester Ship Canal warehouses nearby. However, the G.F.Milnes Company, contracted to build the car bodies during the boom time for the British tramcar industry, seemed unable to meet their promised delivery dates, and their difficulties were not eased by a changed decision on the part of the Salford Tramways Commit-

tee. As the system was not yet ready for electric operation, delay at this stage early in the year did not greatly matter. The Committee had previously selected a livery from a range of 'primary colours' supplied by Milnes and had chosen maroon (chocolate) and cream, with the title 'SALFORD CORPORATION TRAMWAYS' in gold and blue letters on a cream background, together with the borough coat-of-arms on the sides and ends of each car. They had made various other decisions regarding, for example, the number of lamps, the style of destination indicators, etc., and had agreed that the cars would be equipped with the 'New London Dry Seat' on the open top deck, which device was claimed to allow rain water to run off rapidly, the seat remaining dry even in wet weather. All these decisions having been duly communicated to G.F.Milnes & Co., on the 20th March 1901 the Committee had visited the Birkenhead works to inspect the first completed car. Whilst there, the members had been greatly impressed by a car being built for Nottingham, which differed from the type ordered by Salford in that it offered additional seating accommodation (55, as against 45 on the Salford order) by virtue of its extended top deck and reversed stair arrangement, which also provided a more protective canopy above the driving platforms. Evidently, at this date 20 cars were in an advanced state of construction, for it was resolved that the remaining 80 cars of the original order would have the top-deck ends and staircases built in a similar fashion to the Nottingham car, at an additional cost of £35 per car. Further deliberations took place in subsequent meetings of the Tramways Committee, resulting in terms being agreed in June 1901 for alterations to the first 20 cars so as to convert them to the same design. As these were already under construction, and as modifications were therefore not so easily effected as when starting from scratch, the additional amount required by Milnes for such alterations was to cost £50 per car.

The track layout at St.Mary's Gate in Manchester reflected the inter-running disagreement with the neighbouring authority. This June 1901 picture shows the junction ready for electric operation before the road setts had been replaced. Deansgate runs from left to right, and the photographer was looking directly into Blackfriars Street, where the Salford tramcars were forced to terminate some 150 yards from Deansgate at the bridge over the River Irwell. Although both corporations had chosen the same track gauge and method of current collection so that inter-running would have been possible from the outset, Manchester did not include in this junction any direct connection between Blackfriars Street and St.Mary's Gate.

By August 1901, with electric services hopefully scheduled to commence in October, the delivery of new cars became much more urgent. The G.F.Milnes Company promised delivery of 20 cars by mid-September. Ernest Hatton thought that these 20 cars would be sufficient to open the Higher and Lower Broughton routes by electric traction. The Tramways Committee optimistically resolved that, if Milnes could supply an extra 10 cars, the Pendleton route would be opened simultaneously. Unhappily, Milnes under further pressure, revised their delivery dates and said that Salford would have only 6 cars by the end of September, 14 in October, 20 in November, and 10 in December, this total being 50, half the full order, the remaining 50 to follow in 1902. Milnes' inability to supply the cars more quickly was understandable. The year 1901 proved to be the peak period for the production of tramcars in this country, five builders supplying some 3000 vehicles. Of that total, the G.F.Milnes Company produced 701, the highest figure ever reached.

However, the delay in delivery had allowed work to proceed unimpeded on the car depot in Frederick Road, and at the end of August two bays of the new shed were ready to receive vehicles. The first electric tramcar body from Milnes arrived on Saturday, the 14th September. After the weekend, it was fitted with its electrical equipment and prepared for trial runs and driver-training duties. The cost for the complete tramcar had totalled £575. The first test of the new vehicle took place late at night along Seaford Road on Wednesday, the 18th September 1901, with more intensive trials on the following day. The Blackfriars Bridge to Kersal (Higher Broughton) route was almost ready for operation by electric tramcars, and it was hoped that several more cars would be ready for testing and driver-training within a few days. Rivalry with Manchester was strong, settlement of the dispute seemed as far away as ever, and as Manchester's electric trams were already operating along Bury New Road as far as the Grove Inn, it was decided to compete and salvage civic pride by inaugurating electric traction on the Higher Broughton route as speedily as possible. To this end, workmen erecting the overhead wires on the Pendleton route were switched to the Higher Broughton line, and worked day and night shifts to complete the task. Because of the uncertainty of the likely opening date, no formal ceremony was planned, and it was agreed that such celebrations would attend the opening of the Pendleton route, which, in other circumstances, might have seen the first electric services.

By the 23rd September four complete cars were ready, and were used in and around the depot on driver-training duties. The General Manager was impatient - he needed only two more cars to be able to open the first electric service. The Higher Broughton route underwent its statutory Board of Trade Inspection (by Colonel Von Donop) on Friday the 27th September, and on the following Monday, Mr.Trotter, also representing the Board of Trade, pronounced its electrical equipment satisfactory. In anticipation of approval being gained, it had been announced that electric operation would commence on Tuesday, the 1st October, cars running between Blackfriars Bridge and Kersal, and from Blackfriars to the new car shed on Frederick Road, via Sussex Street and Lower Broughton Road.

In the event, the long-awaited opening of the Higher Broughton route, with the six required cars, did not take place until Friday, the 4th October 1901. The new cars followed the route taken by the horse trams, but with one exception - the single-line temporary track in Upper Camp Street used by the inward-bound horse trams, although replaced by new permanent track, was not used by the electric vehicles. Some six weeks earlier it had been decided to equip a double line in Great Cheetham Street. Thus, both inward and outward cars travelled to Bury New Road via part of Great Clowes Street and Great Cheetham Street. Whether or not the Upper Camp Street line was ever fitted with overhead equipment is not certain. It was recorded that permanent junctions had been effected with the lines on the main roads at each end as recently as August, but that Upper Camp Street would "*not be utilised for electric traction at the present time.*" However, in order to provide some sort of service along that portion of Bury New Road which lay between the Manchester boundary and the junction with Great Cheetham Street, the Salford Manager contemplated using four horse cars on a service between the Grove Inn and Kersal, but then rejected the idea on the grounds that the slower horse cars might impede the progress of the electric vehicles on the overlapping portion of the route. Instead, he decided that the horse trams freed from the Higher Broughton route would be used on a Weaste to Regent Bridge route, thereby offering a connecting service to the

The construction of the Frederick Road tramway depot proceeded in readiness to receive the first electric cars. Track-laying inside the building included work on inspection pits. Three tracks could be reached through each doorway. The first two bays, as seen in this picture, were ready by September 1901.

The first electric tram route opened with six cars runnning between Blackfriars Bridge and Higher Broughton on the 4th October 1901. The municipal boundary point then saw both horse and electric trams reversing in the middle of the bridge. In this view, passengers are boarding car number 2, which is not yet fitted with route boards or enamel destination plates.
(Photo A.Astle.)

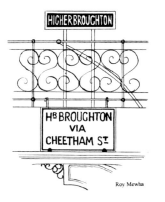

Roy Mewha

Manchester electric cars at Regent Bridge and covering that portion of Regent Road which had lacked any form of service since the start of the dispute.

The route from Blackfriars Bridge to Frederick Road (then called Walness Road) via Sussex Street, though used by electric cars travelling to and from the new car shed when entering or leaving service, remained under operation by horse trams from the Lower Broughton Road depot, partly because new vehicles were still in short supply, and partly because the numerous horse-trams on the short but frequent service on the inner portion of the route, plus those on the longer run to 'The Cliff' (a destination on Lower Broughton Road beyond Cromwell Bridge) might have interfered with the electric car service.

By the 12th October a total of 14 electric cars had been delivered. As the bodies arrived at the Frederick Road Depot, they were united with their electrical equipment by men working under the supervision of Mr.F.Taylor, representative of the Westinghouse Company, whose task it was to ensure that all vehicles were tested and operated satisfactorily. The General Manager reported that six cars were used to provide the regular services on the Higher Broughton route, plus an additional 'relief car' in the 'rush hour.' He noted that 12 horse-trams had been needed on this route before conversion. He proposed to use two more electric cars to run from Kersal to the Grove Inn, connecting with the Manchester cars, just as he had contemplated with the horse trams, and he duly began such a service with ten-minute frequency on the 14th October. This new shuttle-service of cars from the Manchester boundary meant that the portion of Bury New Road beyond Great Cheetham Street had a five-minute frequency as far as Kersal Bar. Receipts per car on this service were said to be £2.1s.10d on the first day, as compared with £6.10s.0 per car on the first opened lines.

On the 21st October 1901, Ernest Hatton began his Weaste to Regent Bridge service of horse cars at a fare of one penny for the whole journey. On the same day, another new horse-tram service began, running from Blackfriars Bridge via Chapel Street and The Crescent, along Cross Lane to its junction with Eccles New Road. (The earlier and similar service, begun in June, travelled via Oldfield Road and Regent Road to Trafford Road.)

In the meantime, work on the Pendleton and Irlams O'Th'Height route was proceeding apace, and these lines had their official inspection on the 15th November. Another six-and-three-quarter miles of single-track had been completed between February and October 1901, to add to the seven or so miles constructed in 1900, and, although other lengths had been laid,

because of the delay in obtaining castings, most of the junctions elsewhere had been left out, a state of affairs of which Ernest Hatton was only too conscious, and which he hoped to remedy as soon as possible.

However, as the Broughton and Pendleton lines were now complete, the Tramways Committee decided to hold a civic banquet to mark the official launch of the electric tramways on the occasion of the opening of the latter route, as soon as a sufficient number of new tramcars had been received to enable operation to commence.

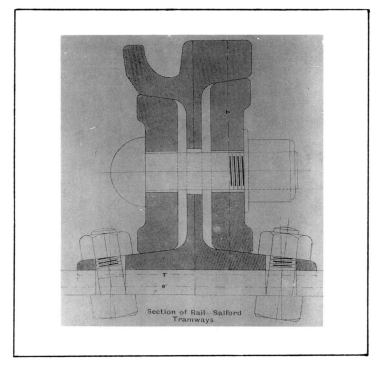

Section of Rail. Salford Tramways.

The formal opening of the Salford electric tramway system took place on the 20th November 1901, on the occasion of the inauguration of the route to Pendleton and Irlams O'Th'Height. Decorated cars drew up in Chapel Street, opposite the Town Hall in Bexley Square, to receive the guests. The Mayor may be seen on the platform of the leading car. Despite heavy rain, crowds turned out to witness the event. An early observer said that the electric tramcars looked 'like elephants tied by their trunks to a clothes line.'

The Celebrations And Official Opening Of The Pendleton Route

The formal opening ceremony of the Salford Tramways took place on Wednesday, the 20th November 1901. Six of the new electric tramcars, "handsomely decorated with flowers, evergreens, and flags," according to the local press report, drew up in Chapel Street opposite the Town Hall in Bexley Square. Despite incessant heavy rain, large crowds had assembled to witness the event. Members of the Tramways Committee and their guests boarded the cars, and the Mayor, accompanied by Alderman Linsley and Ernest Hatton, "set the first car in motion amid ringing cheers."

Amongst the 140 guests were civic dignitaries from adjoining towns, including some from more distant areas, such as Alderman Clegg, Chairman of the Sheffield Tramways Committee. Also attending were Mr.G. Hill (contractor for the overhead equipment), Mr.W.Southern (builder and contractor for the new car depot), and Mr.J.Holt (architect of the new electricity generating station.) Ernest Hatton, accompanied by his then Chief Clerk, G.W.Holford, acknowledged his debt to Liverpool by inviting General Manager C.R.Bellamy. Despite the bitter unresolved deadlock over the inter-running arrangements, the neighbouring city was represented by Councillor Daniel Boyle, Chairman of the Manchester Tramways Committee, and his Deputy, Councillor Wainwright, accompanied by the

General Manager, Mr.J.M.McElroy. The local press reported that one Salfordian asked Councillor Boyle, "*How have you the courage to be seen in Salford?*" Boyle responded disarmingly and diplomatically, "*It is not a question of my courage, but a question of the courtesy of the Salford people.*"

The guests boarded the special cars and were first conveyed along the new route, through Pendleton and as far as the Swinton boundary at Irlams O'Th'Height. There the cars reversed and returned to Broad Street, from which point a diversion was made along Frederick Road for the formal opening of the new car shed, which was said to be "nearly complete." In Seaford Road, the guests assembled around the entrance to one of the bays, whilst the contractors presented to Alderman Linsley a silver key with which to perform the opening ceremony. Alderman Linsley, in thanking the contractors, said that the building, of red brick with stone dressing, would be one of the finest car sheds in the country. When complete it would have cost £50,000, would have eight entrances leading to four bays and twenty tracks, fifteen of which would be equipped with inspection pits for repair work. It would offer accommodation for 180 cars, and would have all the necessary workshops, stores and offices. Across the end of the tracks would be a traverser, which Alderman Linsley referred to as a "travelling table," to facilitate internal working arrangements. At the close of his speech Alderman Linsley announced that there were now "only 90" horse-trams

Guests at the official opening rode on the new tramcars to Irlams O'Th'Height, and before returning to the Town Hall for the celebratory lunch, made a diversion to inspect the new depot on Frederick Road. The building is seen here in its original form. An imposing entrance arch, offices, and further extensions were not constructed until 1907. The centre poles holding up the overhead wiring were much admired for their wrought-iron decorative work and ornamental bases.

working in the borough, and that accommodation for electric cars in the new shed would meet requirements for many years to come.(In the previous year, a second car shed had been contemplated, and a plot of land had been chosen at Weaste, which was not used until 1929. At Frederick Road, an additional bay was constructed at the same time as the main entrance arch and offices, formally opened on the 17th July 1907.)

The guests were then invited to inspect the facilities of the new depot, and afterwards boarded the tramcars to return to the Town Hall, passing on the way the new electricity generating station at Strawberry Hill (Frederick Road), the "gigantic proportions" of which had given rise to much comment. Its sixteen boilers and eight engines were thought by some to be a far more generous provision than the demand was likely to warrant. It was alleged that some of the plant would not be needed until ten or twenty years hence, by which time, claimed the detractors, it would be out-of-date. Being situated alongside the Manchester, Bolton and Bury Canal, coal for the power station arrived by barge, and was lifted by crane into a set of Hodgkinson's patent mechanical stokers, which fired the boilers automatically.(The Hodgkinson company later occupied the Manchester Carriage Company Works premises on Ford Lane, Pendleton.) The work on the generating station was at that time sufficiently advanced to supply power for the Broughton and Pendleton tramway routes.

On arrival at the Town Hall for the celebratory luncheon, it was announced that the whole journey had been completed "with the utmost smoothness, not a hitch occurring throughout the entire route."

In the speeches after lunch, flattering references were made to the various items seen that morning. In accordance with the views of the Board of Trade inspector, centre poles to hold up the overhead wiring had been erected wherever the width of the roadway had allowed, and these were praised for their smart appearance and ornamentation. The contractors were complimented on carrying out work promptly and without undue interference with the horse-tram services, and the handsome appearance of the new cars was duly praised. One speaker could not resist making unfavourable references to the Manchester vehicles - in favour of the reversed staircases adopted by Salford, it was claimed that if a passenger should slip, there would be no likelihood of falling into the roadway, whereas with the design chosen by Manchester, this type of accident was a distinct possibility. Another, referring to the inter-running dispute, claimed that throughout the negotiations Manchester had "displayed a dictatorial and grasping spirit" and had endeavoured "to rob Salford of her just reward for her enterprise." Daniel Boyle had been invited to respond to the toast to the guests. Once again, he was able to reply with tact and diplomacy. He had, he said, admired the beauty of the new tramcars, been impressed by the facilities of the new car shed, and had appreciated the invitation. The differences between the two Corporations were well known, but had he been an outsider, he would have wondered what all the fuss was about, and he hoped common sense would prevail. There was not such a marked difference between them, he thought, as would justify the expenditure of large sums of money in taking their respective cases to Parliament. Both Corporations were standing up for their individual interests, but he felt it should be possible to find a solution which did no wrong to either party. He hoped that the co-operation demonstrated that morning would find an echo in what he referred to as "other places." Boyle's speech received an enthusiastic reception, and, indeed, there did seem little reason why the dispute should not be quickly resolved. The press asked, "*Is it too much to hope that under the genial influence of the Bollinger of Bordeaux the difficulties which have hitherto existed will be removed?*" Sadly, this was not to be the case.

Manchester's Tramway Bill published on the same day as the Salford official opening included proposals for running powers over Salford lines in Bury New Road and Bury Old Road, whilst Salford's Bill requested similar powers over Manchester lines between the Irwell bridges and Deansgate, and along the Manchester portion of Bury New Road. Both Bills suggested that terms should be agreed by the two Corporations, or, failing that, by arbitration, but Salford's Bill also included a proposal for a Joint Board to administer the whole of the Manchester and Salford Tramway systems as a joint undertaking, a novel suggestion which was not to Manchester's taste.

Salford's objections to the Manchester proposals were presented under three main sections :-

1. If Manchester were to have the exclusive right to the Bury New Road route, it would ensure that all the traffic from Salford's Great Cheetham Street district would pass over the city end of the Manchester tramways, thus making a profit for Manchester but depriving Salford of revenue.

2. Salford would not be free to secure the full use of its own routes, but would be required to operate a minimum service over the lines to Deansgate as decided by Manchester.
3. The suggested division of the gross receipts on the city ends of the lines would ensure that Manchester secured not the average profit over the whole system, but a higher one from the busiest portions of the routes.

Unhappily, agreement seemed as far away as ever, and the dispute was destined to be prolonged and acrimonious.

The cover of the menu card at the luncheon to celebrate the formal opening of the electric tramways. Guests at the luncheon included the Chairman of the Manchester Tramways Committee and Mr.C.R.Bellamy, the Liverpool General Manager, with whom the Salford Manager enjoyed a close working relationship.

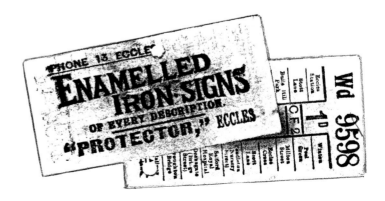

The New Electric Tramcars

By December 1901 thirty of the first 100 electric tramcars were in service. The electric car journey from Blackfriars Bridge to Irlams O'Th'Height took 18 minutes, as against 30 scheduled for the horse-trams. Passengers bound for Swinton or Pendlebury had to change vehicles at The Height and complete their journey by horse-tram. Hopes of a speedy extension of the electric service to these districts suffered a set-back when it was decided that the lines constructed by the Carriage Company would have to be re-laid. Although the Pendlebury line dated only from 1898, tests revealed that the foundations were not strong enough to carry the weight of the electric cars, and the required reconstruction meant that it would be 1903 before electric cars could run to Swinton.

Car number 26 stands in Bolton Road, Irlams O'Th'Height, following the formal opening of this route. The first electric cars were equipped as here with a 'cow-catcher' type lifeguard, soon replaced with the more usual swinging-gate, which cut off the power if activated by any obstruction on the road surface.   (Photo courtesy Salford Local History Library.)

The electric cars weighed over 7 tons each. They had seats for 22 inside and 33 on top, total 55. The facing longitudonal seats in the lower saloon, covered with strips of pale-blue Wilton carpet incorporating the 'SCT' monogram, offered some 18 inches per person (as against 16 on the horse-trams) when the car was full. Top deck passengers enjoyed reversible 'garden-seats,' arranged to give eight double-seats along one side, and seven doubles along the other, with single seats at the stair-heads and alongside the trolley mast. The interior design resembled the Liverpool cars. Despite the official seating capacity, it was not long before the Tramways Committee, having collected evidence from other undertakings, decided that the cars be licenced to carry a maximum of 75. This total, which included provision for a number of standing passengers, had been reached by increasing the top-deck capacity to 35 (converting the two stair-head single seats to doubles), plus 9 standing, together with another 9 standing on the lower deck in addition to the 22 seated. It was firmly announced that any conductor allowing more than the stipulated number of standing passengers would be severely disciplined. Some twenty years later, opinion viewed with alarm the possibility of standing passengers on the top deck. In external appearance, the cars were attractively finished, and it was said that they provided "an agreeable contrast to the now-antiquated horse cars." Facing outwards from each end of the top deck was an internally-illuminated box with a roller-blind destination indicator. This had been patented by the British Electric Car Company, newly established in nearby Trafford Park, just across the road from the Westinghouse. Their new patent indicator box became almost universal on British tramways. The device allowed rolling stock to be used in any part of the system. and was a major advance on the rather inflexible method of painting destinations and routes on the sides of vehicles, which had restricted the horse-trams to particular routes.

On the ends of the cars, just above the platform, appeared the legend 'SWING THE POLE THIS WAY,' accompanied by a direction arrow. This was necessary because the power cable ran from the trolley head through the pole, and down via the trolley mast. Although the trolley pole could be rotated fully, it was essential to remind the guard to swing the pole only in the same half-circle to avoid the danger of twisting the cable. Thus the direction arrows at each end of the car pointed to the same side.

As further electric vehicles arrived, sales of tramway horses rendered redundant by the opening of the first routes began. In December 1901, 170 animals were disposed of at prices ranging from £3-10s.0d to £26.

Tramway Employees

By the end of 1901 the Tramways Department employed a total of 648 workers. This figure included 56 electric car drivers and 57 conductors based at the Central Car Depot in Frederick Road. For the horse trams, there were still 66 drivers and 72 conductors working from the Heyworth Street Depot at Weaste, 25 drivers and 25 conductors at Pendleton, and 12 drivers and 13 conductors at the Lower Broughton Road Depot. Some of the Weaste Depot employees were listed as 'extra men,' and the number of regular drivers and conductors based there appears to have been only 50 each. The number of 'pointboys' was 19. A double-shift system for the traffic staff meant a working period of 8½ hours per man per day.

The General Manager's salary, which had been £240 per annum when appointed in 1899, had risen to £400. Two employees who were to become future General Managers were already on the payroll. G.W.Holford, then aged 30, had been appointed to the position of Chief Clerk in March 1901 at a salary of £160 per annum. and J.W.Blakemore, aged 24, who had been taken over from the Carriage Company in April 1901, was a clerk with a wage of 29 shillings per week.

C.H.Chester, aged 45, and F.South, 43, superintendents respectively of the Weaste and Pendleton horse-tram depots, received £250 per annum, but G.P.Jones, 48, superintendent of the smallest horse-tram depot at Lower Broughton, received only £2-15s-0d per week. After the withdrawal of the horse-trams, C.H.Chester became the Traffic Superintendent, second only to the General Manager, but his salary fell to £200 per annum.

Ticket Inspectors enjoyed a wage of £2 per week. 'Motormen,' drivers of electric tramcars, were paid at the rate of 6d. per hour, rising to 6½d. after one year, whilst their conductors were paid 5½d. per hour, rising to 6d. Applicants for appointment as motormen were expected to be aged not less than 25 years, and to be at least 5 feet 8½ inches tall. Conductors wishing to be trained as motormen could apply after 12 months' approved service. Comprehensive instructions regarding the conduct and duties of motormen and conductors were drawn up, printed and issued to each employee. Amongst the regulations governing behaviour of the staff, was one which read : "'Larking' on the cars is strictly prohibited."

Uniform was provided, and car crews were further identified by brass numbers fixed to collars. Until 1915, motormen were allocated the odd numbers, and conductors even numbers. White covers for the caps were provided to be worn in summertime, which officially began on the 1st May. Clean and tidy dress was mandatory, and anyone failing to reach the required standard could be sent home.

One unusual feature of the Salford and Manchester tramways was the employment of a third, junior member of crew - the trolley boy. The trolley boy was normally stationed on the rear platform of the car, and his general role was to assist passengers whilst the conductor collected fares. He was expected to call out stages on the journey, ring the bell for starting and stopping, supervise boarding and alighting, turn the trolley pole, and wind destination indicators at termini. It was a common belief amongst travelling

Salfordians that only the cheekiest and most impudent youths were ever offered this sort of employment. The management took a different view, and instructed the boys to be 'civil and obliging' at all times on pain of instant dismissal. To ensure that the trolley boys earned a reputation for 'smartness in conduct and appearance,' attendance at drill and physical exercise sessions in the depot yard was compulsory. On these occasions, the boys would be paraded and inspected military-style, and at one time the youth judged to be the smartest and cleanest in appearance was rewarded with the easiest turn of duty.

The required attendance of the trolley boys at the drill and physical training sessions led to a complaint from the motormen and conductors, who protested that the boys should not be withdrawn from the cars at busy periods. The criticism met with no sympathy from the General Manager, who responded that the staff of most other tramway undertakings had to manage without any assistance whatsoever.

More Early Routes

Track re-construction was as yet concentrated within the city boundary, and as castings and special steel-work became available, Ernest Hatton was able to deploy his workforce to complete the junctions which he had previously left out. Consequently, the special trackwork for the Cross Lane and Regent Road junction was first laid out for a trial in the permanent way yard on Strawberry Road, and then fixed in position on its real location by a force of 200 men early in December 1901. Within a few months, however, Hatton had borrowed certain sections for use elsewhere on the system, and had re-designed the junction. The sale of the New Barns Racecourse site off Trafford Road had made unnecessary the conversion of the Goodiers Lane horse-tram line, which was now to be abandoned, and the General Manager reported that he was to re-plan the layout at Cross Lane to take account of new routes. This was to become the famous 'Grand Union' junction.

On the 5th January 1902 the General Manager was able to open a second, more direct route to Kersal via the upper reaches of Great Clowes Street, joining Bury New Road at Bella Vista, the worries about subsidence at that point having been temporarily resolved. In addition, cars were now able to run past the previous Kersal terminus at Moor Lane, as far as the Prestwich boundary. On the other side of the borough, it was announced that work on the Eccles New Road line as far as Ladywell was nearly complete, but that as the agreement with Eccles had not yet been signed, the Salford Corporation could not extend the track across the boundary to Eccles Cross. It was also revealed that the electricity department was taking advantage of the tramway installations by placing arc lamps on the top of the tramway poles along Blackfriars Road, Chapel Street and Broad Street.

By the 10th February 1902 a total of 50 electric cars had been delivered. It was evident that frequent visits were made to the Milnes works to try to speed delivery, and the Tramways Committee requested that "*the report of the person inspecting the cars in progress of construction at Birkenhead to be submitted on each occasion.*" Ernest Hatton reported that he hoped to be in a position to close the Lower Broughton Road horse-tram depot by mid-April, and that he would also be able to close the Weaste horse-tram depot if the Eccles New Road route to Eccles Cross could be operated by electric cars. Horse trams would still be required between Eccles and Peel Green, but these could be supplied from the Pendleton depot, which serviced the Eccles Old Road and Swinton routes. By March, however, he regretted to report that the contract for the supply of new tramcars was "far from being completed," but in the following month, more optimistically, he was able to open two new routes, each two-and-three-quarter miles long. Although the new lines had not yet been inspected, the Board of Trade had been indulgent, and had agreed that services could commence at Salford's own risk pending approval. Thus, on Friday, the 4th April 1902, two new services began from Blackfriars Bridge, one to Trafford Bridge, via Chapel Street and Oldfield Road, at a through fare of 1½d.; and the other to Weaste (Cemetery Road) along Eccles New Road. Eccles Council had delayed completion of the work over the further section from Ladywell to Eccles Cross. Nevertheless, progress was celebrated by the running of a decorated car as far as Ladywell Sanatorium on the Salford side of the boundary.

The horse-tram route along Eccles New Road and Regent Road, begun in October 1901 to connect with the Manchester cars at Regent Bridge, ceased as soon as the electric cars began running via Oldfield Road to Weaste, leaving the portion of Regent Road between the bridge and Oldfield Road without a service once again. The opening of the two electric routes on the 4th April also enabled the General Manager to remove horse-cars from Blackfriars Bridge entirely, thereby deflecting the press criticism that it had been "*scandalous that the horse trams had to turn there, so narrow was the*

Horse-trams from the Pendleton Depot continued to provide the connecting services from Irlams O'Th'Height to Swinton and Pendlebury until the electric route was extended in 1903, through passengers having to change vehicles at this point. Car P 13 waits under the electric wires for Swinton passengers arriving on the next electric tram from Pendleton.

road." A great source of annoyance was thus removed, though the congestion was not eliminated. The General Manager could now afford to offer 400 horses for sale. Horse-trams continued to work the Lower Broughton route, but they started from Victoria Bridge. Elsewhere, the only remaining ones were on the Eccles Old Road to Peel Green, and the Irlams O'Th'Height to Swinton and Pendlebury sections. Not until the 15th April did Salford secure agreement from Eccles to begin relaying the old horse-tram track on the short length between Ladywell and Eccles Cross. In the meantime, work had concentrated on finishing touches to the Lower Broughton line to Cromwell Bridge, which was almost complete, but which would continue to be operated by horse-trams because of the continued shortage of electric cars. Colonel Von Donop inspected the Lower Broughton line (together with the Weaste and Trafford Road sections) on the 18th April, and was told that the Tramways Committee was "handicapped by want of cars."

Despite protests, Salford Council announced that it was not prepared to commence work on relaying the Swinton and Pendlebury lines until the arbitration award for their purchase from the Manchester Carriage & Tramways Company had been settled.

Work on the Lower Broughton line had proceeded speedily in an effort to open the route with electric tramcars in time for the Easter meeting at the Manchester Racecourse. The last race meeting at the New Barns estate near Trafford Road had taken place in 1901, after which the land had been acquired by the Manchester Ship Canal Company for the construction of the large new Number 9 Dock. The racecourse had then been re-located within a loop of the river at Castle Irwell, near Cromwell Bridge, and, as was usual during race meetings, thousands of patrons were expected to arrive at the main Manchester railway stations requiring local transport to the entrance gates. On Easter Monday and Tuesday, 31st March and 1st April 1902, traffic to the new racecourse had been worked temporarily by electric tramcars, after which the new cars had been removed for the opening of the Trafford Bridge and Weaste routes. But on Friday, the 2nd May 1902, exactly one year after Salford had operated its first municipal service of horse-trams, Ernest Hatton had a sufficient number of electric cars in stock to enable him to open the Lower Broughton route with a 7½ minute service. From Victoria Bridge, close by Manchester's Exchange Station (which, like Manchester Racecourse and Manchester Docks, was actually in Salford), the cars travelled outwards via Broughton Bridge and Lower Broughton Road to its junction with Great Cheetham Street West at the Griffin Hotel, some 500 yards short of the former horse-car terminus, returning via Sussex Street and Great Clowes Street. The horse-trams on the Lower Broughton route, which for some weeks during the reconstruction had gone only as far as the junction of Lower Broughton Road and Frederick Road at St.Boniface's, were now removed, and there were no horse-trams using the lines at the Victoria or Blackfriars bridges at the Manchester boundary. Only those working the Eccles Old Road route to Peel Green from Pendleton, and those operating from Irlams O'Th'Height to Swinton and Pendlebury now survived.

Horse-trams made a brief and unscheduled re-appearance in Broughton,

The electric tramcar route along Lower Broughton Road terminated near Cromwell Bridge, opposite the Griffin Hotel, whereas the horse-trams had continued further to a point sometimes known as 'Broughton Spout' but designated 'THE CLIFF.' The electric tramcars also displayed the same terminal destination for the shortened route until 1907, when it was altered to the more specific 'CROMWELL BRIDGE.' Car 16, carrying the earlier destination display, stands outside the Griffin Hotel in 1902 ready to resume its return journey to Blackfriars Bridge.

though not for passenger traffic, when the Manchester Carriage & Tramways Company, anxious to transfer cars stored at their Cheetham Hill Depot to the Higher Broughton premises in Knoll Street, asked permission for their vehicles to pass over the Salford lines in Bury New Road early in May 1902. Permission was granted on condition that the cars were moved in the early morning so as not to interfere with normal time-table workings.

One week after the opening of the Lower Broughton route, on the following Friday, the 9th May, Ernest Hatton was able to institute a five-minute service of electric cars to Eccles Cross. The Mayor and Chairman of the Tramways Committee travelled on a special car and invited the Mayor of Eccles to join them on the return journey. Thereafter, alternate cars travelled to Eccles via Oldfield Road or Cross Lane, the Trafford Bridge service alternating in a similar manner. On Trafford Road, the lines continued to the centre of the swing bridge across the Manchester Ship Canal, but were not as yet used. It was hoped that very soon they would be continued on the Stretford side by Manchester Corporation to connect with the Trafford Park tramways and link with their Old Trafford lines.

In June 1902, in response to protests, Ernest Hatton arranged for some cars on the Weaste service to traverse the whole length of Regent Road to connect with the Manchester cars at Regent Bridge, thus re-instating a service which had vanished some two months earlier when the horse-trams had been withdrawn from that route. At about the same time, on the other side of the borough he abandoned the Bury New Road shuttle service which had run from the Manchester boundary at the Grove Inn to meet the service cars at Great Cheetham Street. He announced that this had proved unremunerative, and that there had been no complaints since the cars had been taken off.

Interviewed by a local journalist in July 1902, Hatton was able to report that he now had 75 electric cars available for service, and that only 12 horse cars remained.

The electric tramcars reached Eccles Cross in May 1902, Car 53 stands at the then terminus in Eccles, having reversed for the return journey to Blackfriars Bridge. A fare table hangs in the window of the lower saloon. The reversible back-rests of the top-deck seats may be noted.

By August 1902, the order for the first 100 electric cars had still not been completed, but it was reported that all 90 then delivered had been in service on a Saturday night in connection with the Coronation celebrations of King Edward VII. Meanwhile, possibly in an attempt to draw attention to the slow delivery of cars from the G.F.Milnes Company, and to attract future orders, the British Electric Car Company of Trafford Park invited the Tramways Committee to inspect their factory.

The Collins Automatic Point-Turner

Mr.Henry Collins, a tailor with premises near the corner of Chapel Street and Oldfield Road, had been intrigued by watching an "acrobatic points-boy" at work at the junction near his shop. The hazardous activities of this tramway employee caused him to give thought to a less-dangerous way of working, and in June 1902 he and his son Charles had patented their first automatic point-turner, a mechanical system which was a fore-runner of the electrical method which was later adopted. This early device consisted of pedals fitted on the driver's platform, which, when depressed, allowed a six-inch-diameter wheel, normally held above the rail by a spring, to drop into a new middle rail, twelve feet long, fixed at spots where points were located. This wheel could be moved to one side or the other, according to the direction required, to exert pressure in a groove. Connections through underground piped levers moved the tongue of the point, and also acted via the tramway standard on the overhead wire 'frog,' which was normally worked by the points-boy operating a rope pull. A demonstration was arranged, and it was announced that the device would be on view at the Tramway and Light Railway Exhibition in London. It was to be manufactured for the patentees at the works of Thomas Oliver, North George Street, Salford.
A trial, said to be successful, was held at the rear of Frederick Road Depot, and some observers urged the adoption of the system. Being cautious, the Tramways Committee agreed that a sample could be fitted at Mr.Collins'

expense at one junction and on one car. It was estimated that the cost of the rail connections and overhead 'frog' would be £50, together with another £20 for fitting 'direction pedals' on one tramcar.
The Tramways Committee subsequently considered the cost of alterations to the track and overhead wiring, together with the fitting of the extra equipment on all existing cars, and on new cars yet to be ordered. The General Manager estimated that the outlay would have to be some £3700, and, although there would be eventual savings on wages, the then current expenditure of 20 shillings per week on each of the 18 or 19 points-boys stationed at major junctions, amounted to less than £1000 per year. Mr.Collins was therefore informed that no contract would be awarded immediately.
Despite the alleged success of this early demonstration, it was Collins' subsequent patent which came to be favoured by Manchester and Salford, and which was installed at many junctions, making the 'points-boys' redundant. Collins' later development proved far less cumbersome and required no adaptation of the tramcars. The improved version allowed the driver of an electric car to control the points by either taking power, or coasting with power shut off, as the trolley wheel passed under a 'skate' in the overhead wire on the approach to a junction. The usual method was for a driver to approach with caution, coasting if the car was to go straight ahead, but using low power if taking the curve. If the points were already set for the selected route, the point-tongue would remain motionless, but if a change was required, the driver could look ahead to see the tongue move. A local firm, the Forest City Electric Company, manufactured the device, and their name, together with the words 'Collins Automatic Point Turner,' could be read on the metal plate installed by the rails.
At junctions where this device was not fitted, or if it failed to work, the guard or driver, or more usually the trolley-boy, would have to leave the car to lever the tongue over manually, using the point-iron which was carried on every car.
Crews evidently became used to the working of the automatic points fairly quickly. The first examples, not from Collins, were installed in 1906 at several well-used junctions. In 1909 the tramwaymen petitioned the General Manager to ask that when an automatic point failed to function, a boy should be sent from the depot to work it manually until repaired. The Manager told his Committee that this was already the practice, but only at places where a points-boy used to be stationed before the automatic devices

were installed. He felt that it was no great hardship for a conductor or a trolley-boy to carry out this duty when it involved changing a point only some three times per hour.

Advertising On Tramcars

During 1902 the Tramways Committee considered increasing their revenue by accepting offers for the display of advertisements on the exterior panels of the tramcars. The travelling public had been used to seeing external advertisements on the upper-deck panels of the horse-trams, and a continuation of that policy would have caused no surprise. However, the members of the Tramways Committee were very proud of their new electric vehicles, and agreed that any additions to the cars would have to be small, tasteful and inconspicuous. After inspecting some sample plates, which were to be fixed to the top-deck trellis work, the Committee formulated a policy which was to last throughout the tramway era - it was decided that the tramcars would not be defaced by external advertisements.

In subsequent years, small advertising bills were allowed to be fixed to the top portion of inside windows, and occasionally permission was granted for window-stickers to promote some worthy cause, but as a general rule, the only additional displays were those of information for passengers in the form of fare tables or route details.

New Offices And More New Routes, 1902-03

For General Manager Ernest Hatton, 1902 continued to be a very busy year. The offices on Chapel Street and Lupton Street quickly proved inadequate, and he was able to secure a suite of rooms sufficiently large to accommodate all his departmental work in a building on Blackfriars Street. The new General Offices had the advantage of being within a few yards of the main terminus. Here, Hatton proposed to widen Blackfriars Street and to construct a centre loading island with four tracks, though he pointed out that this would not be necessary if Manchester would agree to inter-running. The work of conversion of former horse-tram routes within the then borough boundary became complete with the electrification of the Eccles Old Road route, and a trial trip was made as far as Patricroft Bridge on the 25th

September 1902. Services all the way to Peel Green commenced on the 3rd October, alternate cars travelling via Eccles Old and Eccles New Roads, offering a five-minute frequency on all but the separate portions of the route. With the opening of this service, horse-trams ceased to operate within the former town boundary, and were seen only on the Irlams O'Th'Height to Swinton and Pendlebury sections. By this date, 91 electric cars had been delivered.

Attention now turned to the construction of new tracks in districts which had not previously enjoyed any form of tramway service, and a start was made on laying the rails for the route from Eccles Station to Monton and Winton by way of Wellington Road and Parrin Lane, at the far end of which it was to form a junction with a proposed South Lancashire Tramways line from Worsley, and link also via New Lane with the recently-opened line at Peel Green. However, some delay was to attend work on this route because of the necessity of constructing a new steel bridge over the Bridgewater Canal at Monton.

Elsewhere, on the 8th October 1902 the first rail was laid in Prestwich in the presence of civic officials. Because of the impasse between Manchester and Salford, Manchester had been unable to fulfil its obligations to Prestwich in respect of the construction and working of the tramways, because there was no way by which Manchester cars could reach Prestwich without passing through some portion of Salford. Prestwich had therefore asked for the return of the draft agreement. This must have come as a bitter blow to Manchester Corporation, which had recently spent a quarter of a million pounds to acquire Heaton Park, which lay entirely within the Prestwich boundaries. Instead Salford had agreed to construct the Prestwich tramways in Bury New Road, Bury Old Road and Middleton Road, and to lease them for a period of 21 years. In anticipation of linking with Bury Old Road, Salford had first planned a tramway from Great Cheetham Street along Tetlow Lane and George Street, but later abandoned that scheme in favour of one which would use Leicester Road and incorporate some road-widening and general improvements to the highways in that district. On the completion of the Prestwich arrangement, the Whitefield District Council had agreed to lease tramways in their area, likewise for 21 years. Salford to meet the cost of construction and of the purchase of a length of existing

Continued on page 54

Car 39 in Frederick Road Depot in 1902 displays two unusual features. The decorative wrought-ironwork surrounding the top-deck has been further embellished with filled sections, possibly as an experiment when the Tramways Committee members were considering whether or not to allow small advertisement panels to be fixed on that portion of the tramcars. The notion was not approved. At a later stage, the wrought-ironwork was replaced by sheet-metal panels. The second unusual feature is that the car is mounted on a SB 60 truck from the British Electric Car Company, of Trafford Park. This type of truck was patented by J.W.Wainwright, the Company's General Manager, who claimed it to be 'light, easy-running, and flexible.' It seems likely that the truck had been supplied as a sample in the hope that bulk orders would be placed with the local firm, but, if so, the Company must have been disappointed.

Horse-tram P 4 stands outside the Pendleton office of the Manchester Carriage & Tramways Company on the 2nd October 1902 on the occasion of the last horse-car to Patricroft. The Company title may be seen on the frontage of the building, above the verandah. The driver is William Downsby, aged 74, known as 'Old Bill,' one of the founder-members of the Tramway Workers' Union, and reported to be the oldest and longest-serving driver in England. Electric trams replaced the horse-cars on the Eccles Old Road route on the following day, but horse-trams continued to work on the Swinton and Pendlebury sections for another seven months.

Electric trams replaced the horse-cars on the Eccles Old Road routes in October 1902. Car 74 stands in Liverpool Road at the Peel Green terminus ready to commence the inward journey to Blackfriars Bridge.
(Photo courtesy Salford Local History Library.)

Continued from page 52

tramway belonging to the Manchester, Bury, Rochdale & Oldham Steam Tramway Company. Work proceeded rapidly, and on the 5th December 1902, electric tramcars on the Bury New Road route were able to offer a service as far as Prestwich Station. Two specially-decorated cars ran from Victoria Bridge at 12.30 p.m. to mark the occasion, and carried representatives from both councils along the new route, and then to a celebratory luncheon at the home of Alderman Frankenburg at Kersal. The route opened to the public at 2.00 p.m. with a 7½ minute frequency and at a through fare of 2½d.

Instant criticism came from the Clerk to the Prestwich Urban District Council, who complained that it would be better if the Prestwich service started from Victoria Bridge, as it had done for the special cars, instead of adding to the crushing and general congestion at Blackfriars. The General Manager rejected this suggestion, replying that passengers had been in the habit of joining the cars at Blackfriars, and as the route was worked in conjunction with the Higher Broughton service, it would be confusing if some cars started from a different point.

In the meantime, work had started on the reconstruction of the Swinton tramways. The agreement reached with the Swinton & Pendlebury Council was that Salford would reconstruct the existing Carriage Company track in return for a 21-year lease, at the end of which it would be handed to Swinton free of charge. The double track from Irlams O'Th'Height to Chorley Road and Swinton Church was the first section to receive attention. At the outset, it was intended that horse-drawn omnibuses would be used to maintain a service whilst work was in progress, and in October 1902 Ernest Hatton purchased six second-hand omnibuses for that purpose. W.H.Gaunt, the Trafford Park tramway manager, had attempted to persuade Hatton to buy the four vehicles formerly used on the Pendleton to Trafford Park service, but in asking £30 each he evidently over-estimated the amount Salford was prepared to pay, and the purchases were made elsewhere. However, at first, instead of using the omnibuses, temporary track was laid alongside the sections being relaid so that the horse-trams could continue to operate. It was expected that the first section would be ready for electric traction by February 1903, after which the Bolton Road length to Pendlebury would be reconstructed, the horse-trams being dispensed with altogether before dealing with the Station Road link. In practice the use of temporary track was found to be inconvenient and time-consuming, and a replacement service, using the omnibuses was instituted after all. It met with condemna-

tion by councillors, who alleged that the vehicles placed on the route were "*the worst that could be picked up from the backyards of Manchester.*" The General Manager promised to restore the horse-trams when the line to Swinton Church was completed, and explained that it was chiefly the lack of new tramcars which was preventing the line being worked electrically. The Swinton local press, making the best of a poor situation, commented early in March : "*The return to the old horse cars and the abandonment of the 'buses on the length between Irlams O'Th'Height and Swinton Church has been greatly appreciated. Overhead wires are now being fixed on the Chorley Road section and the opening of the Swinton length of electric service should not be much longer delayed.*"

The track construction as far as Swinton Church was, in fact, complete by the end of January 1903, and work then moved to the Pendlebury line, for which a Provisional Order was required to reconstruct the existing single-line with loops to double-track throughout. Electric tramcars commenced working the first section to Swinton Church on the 7th March 1903 ; on the Pendlebury line as far as Hospital Road on the 25th March ; and the full length as far as the Windmill Hotel was ready by the 3rd April. The Station Road track completed the circle in the following month. Two specially decorated cars ran to Pendlebury on the 3rd April, and later that same day special cars were run to mark the opening of the Bury New Road extension from Prestwich to Whitefield.

The spread of electric tramways throughout Lancashire during this period was evidenced on the 30th March by a demonstration run of tramcars over 32 miles of track from the Liverpool Pier Head via the South Lancashire Tramways system to Bolton, when it was forecast that there would soon be through connection to Manchester.

The Disappearance Of The Horse Trams

Though working only a portion of the Pendlebury route by electric traction by the 25th March 1903, Ernest Hatton decided that the horse-drawn trams and omnibuses should go. His decision brought the inevitable protest from the Swinton & Pendlebury Council, whose members complained that the omnibus service along Bolton Road, Pendlebury, had been withdrawn over a week before the electric cars were ready to run the full distance. Passengers protested that they were charged full fare to the Windmill Hotel, Station Road, but were set down one mile short of their destination. Nevertheless, a sale of the hundred-or-so remaining horses took place at the

The first electric tramcar to Swinton arrived one hour late. Crowds had mustered to witness the event, scheduled for 12 noon on the 7th March 1903, but dispersed during a heavy rain shower. The tramcar arrived at 1.00 p.m., according to the local press, preceded by a motor car 'containing the Clerk to the Swinton & Pendlebury Council.' Whether the late arrival was due to the tramcar or the motor car was not recorded, nor was the reason for the Clerk to travel by motor rather than tramcar. The photograph, taken at the Swinton terminus in Chorley Road, shows both vehicles, with civic officials and members of the Tramways Committee. (Photo courtesy Salford Local History Library.)

Pendleton Church Street Depot on the 24th/25th March, attended by a large number of people interested in the horse trade. A goodly number of buyers were carriage proprietors, some from far afield, and prices realised ranged from £15 to £25 per animal.

The tramcars and omnibuses were not in such great demand - they sold at prices ranging from £4 to £6.10s.0d. A few horse-tram bodies were purchased by Eccles Council, though for what purpose was not clear. One, at least, appears to have been used as a temporary waiting room or shelter at Eccles Cross for a short time. Another was used by Salford for a similar purpose, and was located at the end of Ordsall Lane, by Trafford Bridge, preceding the waiting room and paying-in office which was later constructed on the same spot.

Horse-drawn tramcars thus disappeared from the Salford streets, and thereafter the Church Street premises were not used by the Tramways Department. On the other side of Broad Street, the Pendleton (Ford Lane) Works of the Manchester Carriage & Tramways Company likewise passed into different ownership as the number of horse-drawn vehicles needing maintenance dwindled. The Company itself passed into the hands of the liquidator, only to be re-constituted as a much more modest private hire business with the title 'The Manchester Carriage Company (1903) Limited,' in which guise it survived until the 1980s, latterly offering taxi-cabs for hire from premises which were formerly part of the frontage of its Rusholme horse-tram depot on Wilmslow Road.

In his Annual Report for the year ending 31st March 1903, Ernest Hatton was able to record that all 100 electric tramcars had been delivered, that electrification of the 35 miles of track within the old borough had been completed, together with 8½ miles outside the boundary, and that, of this total, 16½ miles had been newly-completed during the past financial year. A total of 28,150,675 passengers had been carried in the twelve-months (compared with 17,800,000 previously) and receipts had amounted to £144,486 (as against £88,639 in 1901-02).

Salford tramwaymen gained the following concessions :-
1. One week's holiday per year with pay for motormen, drivers, and inspectors.
2. For shedmen, one night's holiday per fortnight, with pay.
3. For 'extra' men, for whom no work was available, payment at the rate of sixpence per hour, with a minimum of not less than four hours per shift, this payment to be made only to those who had been officially notified to attend as 'extra' men at the shed.

An innovation attending the take-over of tramway services by the Corporation had been the issue of tickets, which had not met with universal approval; another was that the new electric cars had fixed stopping places, which the horse-trams had not had, at which passengers could embark or alight. The 'tram-stops' were selected at intervals along each route, and were designated by an enamel sign fixed to the tramway poles.

Financial Matters

By the end of March 1903 the total cost of constructing tramways within the borough had amounted to £390,172, and beyond the borough £50,605. Money was raised by means of long-term loans authorised in the various Acts, and repayable over periods of up to 30 years. For accounting purposes, funds were divided into a revenue account for running expenses and salaries; a redemption account for the repayment of loans; and a capital account showing cumulative expenses.

The cost of construction included items such as bridge and road widening, laying cable pipes, setting back footpaths, and paving, as well as the provision of track, overhead equipment, buildings and vehicles.

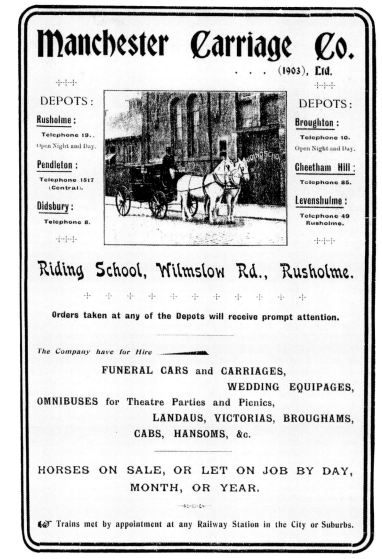

The Manchester Carriage Company was reconstituted in 1903 to carry on a much-reduced business from headquarters in part of the Rusholme premises, concentrating mainly on private hire work. A 1908 advertisement shows that a riding school had been established. Most of the former horse-tram depots had been sold off, but the Broughton premises were retained until the 1920s. Although the advertisement lists six 'Depots,' four, including that at Pendleton, were merely small booking offices.

6

The Settlement with Manchester and Further Expansion, 1903.

The 1902 Parliamentary Bills

The rival Bills presented by Manchester and Salford in 1902 had little result. At the end of the first day's hearing before a Select Committee of the House of Commons in March 1902, the Chairman had remarked that it seemed to be a case which could very easily be settled, and he had adjourned the meeting to enable the parties to confer. He had hoped that they would report back that settlement had been reached. Unhappily, this had not proved to be the case, and on the following day there had been a further clash of opinions. The counsel for the Manchester Corporation had claimed that there was no through traffic worth having to places beyond Manchester, but the Town Clerk of Salford had argued that, although Salford wanted running powers to Deansgate, that was not necessarily where everybody wanted to go, and he instanced Manchester's Piccadilly as being more central. Salford, he said, wanted to connect its main routes with those of Manchester, such routes to be determined, if necessary, by the Board of Trade, so that Salford cars could run into Manchester, and vice versa. The Borough Engineer of Salford said that there should be a through service from "everywhere to everywhere," and that there should be a representative Joint Board to administer the tramway system. Amongst the witnesses called to support Salford's argument was Mr. Glenn, Secretary of the London Street Tramways, who expressed his opinion that any arrangement terminating at Deansgate would be undesirable, whereas through communication would be an advantage for the travelling public. Other supporters of the Salford case included Mr. Henry Crook, Consulting Engineer to the Carriage Company; Mr. A. Nance, General Manager of the Belfast Tramways; and Mr. Marshall Stevens, Managing Director of the Trafford Park Estates Company, all of whom thought that the tramways in the area should be worked as one system, with routes passing through the city centre.

Daniel Boyle replied that Manchester had always been willing to allow Salford to run their cars to Deansgate, and that the present inconvenience to the public could be solved by proposals in the Manchester Bill. He contended that Manchester ought to work the Bury New Road lines because the most important part of that route was near the centre of the city. In addition, Manchester's purchase of Heaton Park and the proposed arrangement with Prestwich had provided further reasons why Manchester should be granted running powers along Bury New Road. Manchester's General Manager, J.M.McElroy, stated that he did not think there was any real demand for through routes as requested by Salford. He did not believe that residents of, say, Eccles on the west, wanted to travel to points to the east of Manchester, and he felt that if Salford passengers were able to alight on Deansgate, "*that would amply meet the public convenience.*"

Surprisingly, at this juncture, counsels for the two Corporations had intervened to say that they had come to an agreement in these terms: "*There shall be an interchange of through traffic, so far as reasonable, upon such routes or portions of routes and upon such terms and conditions as may be agreed upon, or, failing agreement, as shall be settled by the Board of Trade.*" Each Corporation had then withdrawn its application for running powers in the other's territory. The press welcomed the decision to refer the differences to the arbitration of the Board of Trade, and said that the artificial boundary between Manchester and Salford had for too long been a source of annoyance - for all practical purposes, the city and borough formed one great community, and the two Tramways Committees would fail grievously in their duty if they did not work amicably together. An editorial in the 'Manchester Guardian' offered the opinion that the object of the two Committees was "*not merely to secure the largest obtainable profits for Salford or Manchester, but to make the joint tramways service as useful as possible to the community.*" The writer concluded by saying that this aim should not be obscured any longer by "undignified controversies."

Unfortunately, there seemed to be considerable doubt as to what exactly had been meant by the agreement. One Salford councillor thought it meant that if Salford wanted to run cars to points on the far side of Manchester, then consent was first requested from Manchester, and if this was withheld, the request was forwarded to the Board of Trade for an independent decision. A Manchester councillor, on the other hand, interpreted the arrangement as referring only to Salford's wish to run cars as far as Deansgate, and believed that it did not apply to any districts beyond. J.M.McElroy thought it meant that the Board of Trade had to assess and decide on the level of interchange of traffic which would meet the public demand. Such was the confusion that no progress was made, and the situation remained exactly as before. A settlement of the long-standing disagreement appeared likely in September 1902 when Manchester, prevented from using the full length of Bury New Road, decided to offer Salford the right to run the route from Regent Bridge to the Grove Inn, in return for an annual payment equal to the profit Manchester was then earning from its electric cars on that section. Salford accepted the offer, and it seemed as if only the details of the arrangement remained to be worked out. Indeed, the press reported that the dispute was now at an end, and commented, "*The outstanding fact is that for eighteen months two intelligent bodies of men, elected by the ratepayers to look after their interests and to manage local affairs, including tramways, were unable to come to an agreement as to the running of through cars from the centre of one town to the centre of the other.*"

Electric tramcars on the Bury New Road service through Kersal and Prestwich reached Whitefield on the 3rd April 1903.   Car number 4, standing by the railway station, displays a fare table for the Higher Broughton route only.   Two motormen, one presumably from another car, pose for the cameraman. Inside the car may be seen the leather straps for standing passengers to hold, and the curtains on rods at the main windows.   The ventilators, or quarter lights, above the large windows were of plain glass on the early cars, but were later re-glazed with patterned ruby glass, which imparted a hallowed glow to the interior

The Settlement

Reports of an early end to the dispute proved to be premature. Months passed, and the draft agreement was not ratified. Salford began to prepare another Parliamentary Bill, which included requests for further tramway extensions, together with powers to run over and work the tramway from the centre of Trafford Bridge, and to make a junction with Trafford Park tramways. In February 1903 the press commented, "*To the stranger it seems grotesque and childish that the two halves of one city should be divided by an imaginary line impassable by trams.*" The Salford Town Clerk twice wrote to remind the Manchester Council that its offer for Salford to work the Regent Bridge to the Grove Inn tramway had been accepted by his Council, but that the suggested arrangement had not yet been ratified by the Manchester Tramways Committee. This resulted in a series of informal conferences between the two Mayors and the Chairmen of the Tramways Committees. Eventually, 'heads of agreement' were drawn up which appeared to be satisfactory to both sides.

Under the new proposals, Salford was to be granted a 21-year lease, allowing cars to cross the Irwell bridges, to travel the whole length of Deansgate, and to have running powers over the line between Deansgate and the Grove Inn. The rental to be paid by Salford was to be based upon the profit per mile of single track then earned by the Manchester cars operating the Grove Inn route. This sum was calculated to be £1,373 per mile of single track per annum, and as the distance run was to be 6½ miles,

the annual sum would be about £8,900. Under the old disputed arrangement, it had been estimated that Salford would have had to pay a very much larger sum for running from the bridges to Deansgate alone. Manchester was thus to receive a rental for the then unused lines between Deansgate and the Irwell bridges and to gain running powers along Bury Old Road and Middleton Road to reach both sides of its new 'playground' in Heaton Park, for which privilege a rental would be paid to Salford. Manchester further agreed to construct a short length of tramway from Chester Road, Old Trafford, along the Stretford part of Trafford Road to effect a junction with the Trafford Park tramways, which it would endeavour to lease. If successful, powers would be granted to Salford to run across the Trafford Road swing bridge and into Trafford Park. The 'Manchester Guardian' of the 24th February 1903 observed : "*Considered as a bargain, the arrangement has this great merit - that neither party stands to lose by it. ...... We are not without hope that when the two Tramways Committees have found how much more is to be gained by reciprocity than by exclusiveness they will accommodate one another more and more, and will gradually extend the system of inter-communication until it is complete.*"

Before any new services could commence, Manchester had to reconstruct the former horse-tram tracks in Bridge Street and King Street West, and in their portions of Blackfriars Street and Victoria Bridge Street, effecting the necessary junctions with the Deansgate lines. In New Bailey Street,

Salford had already constructed the track, but had to erect the overhead equipment, whilst at the boundaries at Regent Bridge and the Grove Inn it was necessary only to connect the overhead wires. Manchester completed the last piece of work in Blackfriars Street on Saturday, the 30th May 1903, on the morning of which day a trial trip was made using a Salford car which had been newly-fitted with a top-cover.

Car 78 on the depot forecourt in 1902 carries a route board for 'TRAFFORD PARK AND SALFORD DOCKS,' but the fare table reveals the terminus to be Trafford Bridge only. Until October 1905, passengers for Trafford Park had to proceed on foot over the swing bridge to the Park entrance, and there join a gas or electric tramcar of the Trafford Park Estates Light Railway.

Salford's New Routes

Under the new agreement Salford had failed to gain powers to run across Manchester's city centre, and so the idea of long cross-city routes had to be abandoned. Instead, the Tramways Committee adopted the next best course, and arranged some services from districts on one side of the borough to points on the other, all routes passing along part of Manchester's Deansgate. The new arrangements avoided the need for the trams to reverse, or turn, as formerly on the Manchester portion of the routes, thus obviating possible congestion in the city centre streets. The new pattern consisted of eleven routes, counting both directions of the circular service as one route.

Route	To Deansgate Via	From Deansgate Via
1. SWINTON via Chapel Street	Blackfriars Street	Bridge Street
2. PENDLEBURY (reverse of above)	King Street West	Blackfriars Street
3. PEEL GREEN to PRESTWICH	King Street West	Blackfriars Street
PRESTWICH to PEEL GREEN	Blackfriars Street	Bridge Street
4. MONTON via Eccles Old Road	King Street West	Blackfriars Street
5. PEEL GREEN to WHITEFIELD via Eccles New Road	Regent Bridge and Quay Street	Great Ducie Street and Bury New Road
WHITEFIELD to PEEL GREEN	Great Ducie Street	Liverpool Road
6. ECCLES CROSS to GREAT CHEETHAM STREET (Bury Road junction)	Regent Bridge and Quay Street.	Great Ducie Street and Bury New Road
GREAT CHEETHAM ST. to ECCLES	Great Ducie Street	Liverpool Road
7. ECCLES CROSS to KERSAL via Cross Lane	King Street West	Great Ducie Streetand Bury new Road
KERSAL to ECCLES CROSS	Great Ducie Street	Bridge Street
8. TRAFFORD BRIDGE to GREAT CHEETHAM STREET via Bury New Road	King Street West & Oldfield Road	Great Ducie Street
GREAT CHEETHAM STREET to TRAFFORD BRIDGE	Great Ducie Street	Bridge Street
9. TRAFFORD BRIDGE to GREAT CHEETHAM STREET (Albert Park/Great Clowes St.)	King Street West via Cross Lane	Blackfriars Street
GREAT CHEETHAM STREET to TRAFFORD BRIDGE	Blackfriars Street	Bridge Street
10.TRAFFORD BRIDGE to THE CLIFF (Cromwell Bridge)	Regent Bridge and Quay Street	Blackfriars Street
CLIFF to TRAFFORD BRIDGE	Blackfriars Street	Liverpool Road
11. CIRCULAR ROUTE via Frederick Road		
(a) clockwise	Blackfriars Street	Liverpool Road
(b) anti-clockwise	Regent Bridge and Quay Street	Blackfriars Street

[W]hen the terms for running over the municipal boundary were agreed in 1903, all Salford routes passed over part at least of Manchester's Deansgate. In [th]is scene at Pendleton, car 33 is proceeding to Higher Broughton, via Deansgate, whilst the outward-bound car is heading for Peel Green, via Eccles Old [Ro]ad. The former Carriage Company premises are on the left of the picture, whilst to the right may be seen the unwired track leading to the horse-tram [de]pot in Church Street. It may be noted that the third track, a layout retained from horse-tram days, is not yet equipped with overhead wires. Just off the [pi]cture to the right, on the opposite corner of Church Street from the general stores, lies the Horseshoe Hotel, once the home of John Greenwood, Senior.
(Photo courtesy J.M.Lloyd.)

[M]ost of the new services began on Sunday, the 31st May 1903. For almost [tw]o years, first Salford's horse-trams and then the electric cars had been [pr]evented from reaching Deansgate, but with the new arrangements the [pr]ess was able to observe that it seemed rather curious to see Blackfriars [Br]idge without its constant crowd of people waiting for cars. Work on the [St]ation Road link between Swinton and Pendlebury had been completed [sh]ortly before the end of May, and services along this new stretch of track [w]ere inaugurated on the same day that the new Deansgate routes began. [B]ye-laws were revised and published, and it was decided to limit the [nu]mber of standing passengers to six in and six out.

[U]nfortunately, Ernest Hatton found it impossible to implement the full [pr]ogramme immediately. Although the Tramways Committee had placed [or]ders for 50 additional new cars, their arrival was not expected for some [ti]me, and at the start of the new agreement on inter-running, he had an [in]sufficient number of tramcars at his disposal. Consequently, although the [se]ction of track between Eccles Station and Monton Green was ready, it was [no]t opened for traffic until the 15th September. For the same reason, the [Ci]rcular Routes were not put into operation until the 9th October, the same [da]y that new lines in Ordsall Lane and New Oldfield Road were commis-[sio]ned. To save tramcar mileage, and to reduce some duplication of [se]rvices, the route between Trafford Bridge and Great Cheetham Street [(nu]mber 8 in the list above) was quickly altered to run from Trafford Bridge [to] Deansgate only, omitting entirely the Great Ducie Street and Bury New [Ro]ad sections.

But in the new climate of co-operation, Hatton was able to approach his opposite number J.M.McElroy to ask for help. Hatton was anxious to have more cars available immediately, and told his Committee that if Manchester could not assist, he would approach Oldham, where, he said, some electric cars had recently been 'discarded.' But Manchester agreed to lend to Salford the sixteen vehicles (12 single-truck, and 4 bogie cars) which had been used on the Grove Inn to Regent Bridge route. The hire charge was fixed at £7-00 per car per week, the arrangement to last until such time as the delivery of Salford's new cars eased the situation. Thus, at the beginning of June 1903 Ernest Hatton had a total of 116 cars at his disposal, one hundred of his own and sixteen of Manchester's.

Orders For New Cars

Towards the end of 1902 the Tramways Committee had considered the question of purchasing additional tramcars, and had invited tenders for the supply of 50 open-top bogie cars, the new cars to be built in such as fashion as to be capable of being fitted with top-covers later. Seventeen firms responded (16 British, 1 German), but nine were offering to supply parts only. Of the eight firms tendering for the supply of the complete tramcar, prices varied from £709 to £793 per car. A sub-committee was appointed to enquire into the matter, and visits were made to inspect the works of G.F.Milnes, British Thomson-Houston, the British Electric Car Company,

Brush, Dick Kerr, Hurst Nelson, and the Westinghouse, though it was decided to omit a visit to Witting Brothers of London, the eighth firm offering the complete tramcar.

As a result of their investigations, the sub-committee had recommended acceptance of the British Thomson-Houston tender to supply 50 bogie cars at a cost of £748 each, with the proviso that 25 car bodies were to be built by Milnes and 25 by Brush. The aim in splitting the order for the bodies was to gain a more speedy delivery. The Salford undertaking had thus so far ignored their nearest tramcar builder, the British Electric Car Company, except for the use of their patent destination indicators, and some dismay was occasioned by the lack of support for local industry. Marshall Stevens, Managing Director of the Trafford Park Industrial Estate, wrote to the Chairman of the Tramways Committee to urge reconsideration of the order, and the full committee, under pressure from local trades representatives, felt unable to support the sub-committee recommendation. Instead, it was proposed that the Westinghouse tender of £734 per car should be accepted, with 30 bodies to be built by Milnes and 20 by the British Electric Car Company.

The matter was debated again in March 1903. Ernest Hatton presented a case in favour of the British Electric Car Company. He argued that not only did that company employ Salford people, but that theirs had been the only tender for the car bodies to be in complete accordance with the specifications. He believed they could do a first-class job, and reminded the Committee that the firm was close enough at hand in Trafford Park for work in progress to be monitored and inspected at every stage. Hatton thought the Westinghouse equipment was efficient, but extravagant electrically, and defective in armature bearings. British Thomson-Houston equipment was cheaper, he argued, and met specifications, and as the British Electric Car Company price included BTH equipment, he recommended acceptance of

their tender of £720 per car. But it was clear that the Tramways Committee did not have sufficient confidence in the local firm. The wisdom of entrusting the complete order to a small firm like the British Electric Car Company was called into question. It was debatable whether they could deliver on time, and doubts were expressed as to whether they used perfectly dried and seasoned timber. In the absence of agreement, the matter was adjourned for two weeks when a special meeting considered the matter. After what was said to be a very thorough examination of the work and the facilities of the British Electric Car Company, it was agreed to reaffirm the previous recommendation that the tender of the Westinghouse Company be accepted, 20 of the car bodies to be supplied by B.E.C. and 30 by Milnes. Even though only 20 of the bodies were to be ordered from the British Electric Car Company, the trade publication 'Tramway & Railway World' commented: "*Inasmuch as some opposition was raised in the Tramways Committee to the placing of the order, the result should be especially gratifying to the Car Company.*"

The contract was thus placed towards the end of March 1903, with the expectation that the new bogie cars would be delivered in four or five months' time. It was accepted that the new cars would not be available in time for the commencement of the new route pattern, but in order to monitor progress and to urge delivery as speedily as possible, Mr. Clement Stancey, the Depot Superintendent, was deputed to make regular visits to both Milnes and B.E.C., and on each occasion to submit a report to the Committee.

Salford's First Top-Covered Cars

The first Salford electric tramcar to travel over Manchester lines did so on the morning of Saturday, the 30th May 1903, the day before the new

The agreement with Manchester enabled the Salford General Manager to institute a number of long routes connecting districts to the west and north of the system. Car 44 is seen in Liverpool Road, Peel Green, about to reverse for the journey to Whitefield, via Eccles New Road, Regent Bridge, and Deansgate. The off-set position of the trolley mast on the top-deck may be noted. The 'scissors' crossover in the foreground was later reconstructed to leave only the single trailing link, as facing points were considered to be potentially dangerous. Even at this stage, it is clear that the trailing crossover is the one in more general use.

services commenced. It was car number 56 on a trial run, arranged not merely to test out the new lines, but also to check that the car's new top-cover would not cause problems with the overhead wires. Another motive may also have been to show off the new appendage in the rival city, for this was the first top-covered tramcar to appear in Manchester. On the test run were the General Manager and the Chairman, with other members of the Tramways Committee. Once again, there was a connection with the Liverpool General Manager, C.R.Bellamy, for in 1902 it was he who had first experimented with top covers on cars, which, like the Salford vehicles, incorporated the reversed stair. The top-cover fitted was of a style subsequently referred to as the 'Bellamy roof.' It enclosed only the central portion of the upper deck, leaving the ends open. An extra seat was gained by removing the trolley mast, and re-mounting the trolley-pole on the roof, which had to be built strongly in order to carry the weight and to absorb the winging motion of the pole.

Bellamy's developments in Liverpool had been watched with interest, and in March 1903 the Tramways Committee had agreed to the General Manager's suggestion that two or three cars should be fitted with experimental top-covers of the Bellamy type. Covering the top enabled the upper deck to be used in all weathers, and it was claimed that the financial outlay was recovered from extra revenue in only one winter.

The first top-cover was ordered from G.C.Milnes, Voss & Company, of Birkenhead. George Comer Milnes had formerly worked for his father, G.F.Milnes, and had joined with Thomas W. Voss, chief draughtsman, to manufacture tramcar accessories. The unpopularity of the open top-decks of tramcars in wet weather led the partners to concentrate on the supply of top-covers. At this time, Bonomo Magrini had established himself in Liverpool as an agent, developing other people's inventions for commission, and in June 1902 had registered a patent for a tramcar roof which

resembled Bellamy's design for Liverpool. Tramway historian J.H.Price (*'Modern Tramway' 1968, September-December*) is of the opinion that as the so-called 'Bellamy' cover would have infringed the Magrini patent, it may be assumed that the same person was responsible for both, and that Magrini was acting for Bellamy. Whatever the reason, the Milnes Voss Company acquired the sole rights to the Magrini patent, and made special introductory offers to fit up sample cars in the customer's depot, hoping thereby to induce operators to order more.

The first Magrini top-cover for Salford was delivered to the Frederick Road Depot by mid-May 1903 at a cost of £68, and was fitted to car number 56. A second, improved cover followed, equipped with Hall's patent window-raising apparatus, claimed to be the first anywhere, and was fitted to car number 6, the cost having increased to £76. In July, both covers having been carefully inspected, it was recommended that the most desirable features of both should be combined, and that the style of roof on the second cover should be incorporated with the Magrini sides of the first. Milnes Voss responded with an invitation to the Tramways Committee to visit their works, and then proceed to the Wallasey Tramways Depot, where a recently-equipped car, similar to the chosen pattern, could be viewed to assess the final effect. The third cover, combining the approved features of the first two, arrived late in August to be fitted to car number 9, and it was decided to recommend this type for the 17 additional covers it was agreed to order. In September a tender of the British Electric Car Company, of Trafford Park, to supply the 17 extra Magrini covers under licence from Milnes Voss, at £92 each was accepted. The tender from Milnes Voss had been for £118 each. The higher cost of the new covers was to incorporate lighting circuits, ventilators, and window-winders, which latter, it had been decided, were to be operable by the conductor only.

A deputation from Glasgow was reported to have greatly admired the third

Whilst awaiting the delivery of additional tramcars, Salford borrowed 16 Manchester cars in June and July 1903. These were used mainly on the routes to Swinton and Pendlebury. In this view of the junction at Windsor Bridge, Manchester car 189 is heading for Deansgate, preceded by Salford car 21 to Higher Broughton. Another Manchester car is approaching in the distance. The tramway standards were used by the electricity department *to mount their street lights, and The Crescent and Broad Street were amongst those roads first selected for this privilege, though the pole in the foreground, leading to Cross Lane, has not yet been favoured. Gas lamps remain on the pavements. The public houses on the left, either side of the bridge, were the 'Windsor Bridge Inn' and the 'Prince Of Wales Feathers.'*
(Photo courtesy J.M.Lloyd.)

top-covered car.

At the same time that the second sample Magrini top-cover was fitted, the car had also been equipped with an improved destination indicator of the double-line type, which was able to display additional information about the route to be followed. This enlarged destination box was soon adopted as standard equipment for all cars in the fleet, and the single-line boxes of the first hundred cars were quickly replaced with the new versions, ordered from the British Electric Car Company in July 1903. It cost £9 per car for the fitting of the double-line destination box, with associated alterations, on the existing cars, but would add only £4 to the cost of new cars.

The fitting of top-covers increased the seating capacity of the top-deck by one. On the open-top cars, the trolley-mast was off-set so as not to obstruct the central gangway, and had one single-seat beside it, which could now be replaced by the more usual double-seat. On the covered cars, the trolley base was mounted on a strengthened plank on the roof, the current passing through a brass slip-ring in the base to cables inside the car body. The advice

to guards to 'SWING THE POLE THIS WAY' was therefore not necessar on the covered cars, whose trolleys could be rotated on either side withou mishap. As Salford always used the swivel-head trolley, it was possible fo the guards to place the trolley-wheel safely on wires which were nc centrally-placed over the car. This had the advantage that under low bridge the wires could be positioned at the sides of the roads, out of reach of top deck passengers.

Salford also commisssioned the British Electric Car Company to build horse-drawn tower wagon, for overhead line work, at a cost of £90.

The New Bogie Cars And Additional Routes

The first examples of the fifty new tramcars from Milnes and the Britis Electric Car Company began to arrive in August 1903. Members of th Tramways Committee took a trip on one of the new vehicles, riding fron Victoria Bridge to Eccles and thence over the new lines, not yet opened fo

The first top-covered car to be seen in Manchester was Salford's number 56 fitted with an experimental Magrin roof. It was tested over the new Manchester track connecting Blackfriars Street with Deansgate on Saturday, the 30th May 1903, the day before the new services began. The towe wagons in the picture belong to Manchester, and were no doubt in attendance in case the new cove damaged the overhead wiring.

A second Magrini top-cover was fitte to car number 6 in June-July 190. incorporating the luxury of 'Hall Patent Window-Raising Apparatus' an a more informative double-line indicato box. It was agreed to combine the bes features of each cover in a third sampl after which a further 17 were orderee The Magrini covers left the ends of th top-deck open, but offered protectio from the weather to passengers in th centre portion. It was claimed that th covers more than repaid their cost b the extra revenue generated in only on winter.

...horse-drawn tower wagon for overhead line work was ordered from the ...itish Electric Car Company. Years later, the wooden structure was re-...ounted on a motorised chassis.

...ffic, to Monton, then back to Eccles and Peel Green, there reversing to ...ss via Regent Bridge and Deansgate to Prestwich and Whitefield. The ...vellers declared themselves highly delighted with the superior riding ...alities of the bogie car. They congratulated themselves on now possess-...; "some of the finest cars in the country."

...20 cars from the Trafford Park firm were in service by early September, ...d the 'Manchester Courier,' referring to this order, wrote : *"If ever there ...s any doubt as to the ability of the Company to turn out satisfactory cars ...the type required, and within the time specified, that doubt has been ...pelled. The twenty cars ordered from the Company have just been put ...o service, and in point of finish and general excellence of workmanship ...y leave nothing to be desired."* The delivery of the cars from the ...E.C.Company works evidently took place over the Trafford Park tracks, ...ne arrangement being made to draw the cars over the gap in the metals ...ween the end of Trafford Park Road and the Salford lines beyond the ...ing bridge. The Estates Company later submitted a bill to the B.E.C. ...mpany for *"repairing line damaged by your men in dealing with Salford ...rporation cars at Trafford Road entrance."*

...e arrival of the new cars enabled Ernest Hatton to return all but one of ...16 Manchester cars which had been on hire. They had been in use in ...ford for some three months, often appearing on the Pendleton and Irlams ...Th'Height routes. The car which was not returned promptly was Man-...ester number 466, a Brush-built bogie car, which had caught fire due to ...overheated resistance box whilst operating traffic to the races at Castle ...ell on the 5th June. The body of the car was badly damaged, and was ...uilt at Salford's expense by the G.F.Milnes Company for £210, return-

ing to the Manchester fleet in October 1903.

Salford's new bogie cars had been allocated the fleet numbers 101 to 150, 101 to 130 being the Milnes-bodied cars, and 131 to 150 those from B.E.C. Being built to the same design, the two versions were almost identical, and could be distinguished only by careful examination of small items such as corner brackets, or head-stock ends, which bore the characteristic design of their respective makers. Like the single-truck cars, they featured the reversed stair. Their longer bodies offered seats for 77 (32 on the lower deck, 45 on the open top). As delivered, they were equipped with four 25 horse power motors, and were capable of a powerful turn of speed.

The additional cars enabled Ernest Hatton to commence services over the tracks from Eccles Station to Monton Green on the 15th September, where further progress awaited the construction by Eccles Council of a new bridge over the Bridgewater Canal. He was also able to inaugurate his long-planned circular route from the Docks via Manchester and Broughton, together with new services along Ordsall Lane and New Oldfield Road, on the 9th October 1903. The local press, commenting on the Ordsall Lane route, said : *"The cars on this service will open out a district that is densely populated, and it is a route which should prove most remunerative."* The reporter looked forward to an extension of the service into Trafford Park,

which he optimistically forecast would be in a few months' time, but the Ordsall Lane tracks terminated some distance short of Trafford Bridge, and could not be joined until a portion of a new street had been constructed to link with Trafford Road.

In fact, within a few months the Ordsall Lane service (which was a variation on the former Trafford Bridge route to The Cliff via Regent Bridge and Deansgate) was shortened to terminate at the junction of New Park Road with Ordsall Lane, presumably because of poor receipts from the last few yards of track.

With the opening of these additional routes, the total length of tramways worked by the Corporation's 150 tramcars was as under :-

Salford	35.5	miles owned by the Corporation.
Manchester	5.5	miles agreed running powers.
Eccles	6.5	miles leased.
Swinton & Pendlebury	7	miles leased.
Prestwich	3.25	miles leased.
Whitefield	1.75	miles leased.
Total	59.5	miles (single track)

The British Electric Car Company In Decline

Because their Trafford Park premises had never been utilised to full capacity, in order to compete more effectively and to try to gain a larger share of the market, the British Electric Car Company directors had embarked upon a price-cutting policy, which had an effect throughout the industry. The first casualty of this policy was the oldest-established tramcar builder, the firm of G.F.Milnes & Company, which was forced into liquidation, but the B.E.C.Company itself was soon to follow. Trading ceased, and when representatives of the Salford Tramways Committee called at the works on the 2nd December 1903, they were surprised to find it closed. A liquidator was appointed to wind up the business, and he decided that the works could re-open and that contracts already accepted would be honoured. Thus, by the 8th December the Salford Committee had been assured that work on the 17 top-covers had re-started, and that early delivery could be expected.

The original tender submitted by the B.E.C.Company for the supply of the 17 Magrini top-covers had included a sum of £8-0-0 each for the patent rights for Milnes Voss. In fact, Milnes Voss claimed the sum of £5-10s-0d as royalty for each Magrini top-cover for Salford, and said that this was less than their usual charge. Salford paid the royalty direct, and then deducted the sum of £8-0-0 each from the B.E.C. tendered price !

When the 17 covers were delivered early in 1904, it would appear that they were fitted to the most recent arrivals in the fleet, and that the first three cars to have the sample covers were re-numbered at an early stage, so as to bring all the top-covered cars into the 81 - 100 series.

It had been hoped that the British Electric Car Company factory in Trafford Park could have been sold as a going concern, but a buyer failed to materialise, and the works closed. Eventually, along with the G.F.Milnes works, it passed into the hands of the Dick, Kerr group, which later became the United Electric Car Company, whose stated purpose was to reduce outside competition by the removal of 'wild and reckless trading.' The factory was ultimately offered for sale on the condition that it should not be to a firm of tramcar builders.

Fifty new bogie cars were delivered from August 1903. Car 113 is seen in service at Pendleton, with the Carriage Company premises to the left and the former Pendleton Town Hall in the centre distance. The new larger cars were equipped from the outset with the double destination indicator, a it was resolved to replace the single-line boxes on the small cars w similar equipment.

The inauguration of the Circular Route from the Docks via Broughton had to wait until a sufficient number of cars were in stock. The service commenced in October 1903, and one of the small cars, number 74, is seen heading for Trafford Bridge on this service, having just crossed the 'grand union' junction at Cross Lane. The hansom cabs waiting on the left of picture were a regular feature of the Trafford Road Cab Stand at the s of Stowell Memorial Church.

Cross Lane's 'grand union' junction is seen again in this early commercial postcard. There were double tracks round each of the four corners, as well as directly across the junction from each road. Crossovers were provided nearby in all four directions, with a third line, or lay-by, for short workings, in Eccles New Road to the left. Point-boys and tramway inspectors were always in evidence at this important junction. Three inspectors may be seen in this picture, whilst a point-boy stands near his hut by the tram-stop on the right. A policeman to control traffic is posted by the ornate centre-pole, as car 63 with its new double indicator approaches. The centre-poles proved hazardous for increased motor traffic in later years, and a replacement programme was begun as early as 1908. This one was removed about 1912. The 'Ship Hotel' and the 'Regent Theatre' (later the 'Palace') are on the left of the picture, with the tower of the Lancashire Fusiliers' Cross Lane Barracks in the centre distance.

Cross Lane, Salford.

VIEW OF THE HEIGHT

Magrini top-covers were fitted to a total of 20 four-wheel cars. Number 85 is passing along Bolton Road at Irlams O'Th'Height on its way to Pendlebury. The third track lay-by may be noted. A cabmen's shelter is seen on the extreme left, and centre left (behind the horse and cart) is the building at the end of Claremont Road which was once the toll-collector's house for the Irlams O'Th'Height turnpike. Beyond the tramcar, the road divided, Swinton to the left, Pendlebury to the right.

(Photo Charles Wilkinson.)

7

Further Expansion
and the Trafford Park Tramways, 1904 - 05.

In one small matter, the year 1904 did not begin well in Salford. In January there was a fire at the Electricity Generating Station in Frederick Road, and the trams had to be run using power supplied by rival Manchester, but in other respects the outlook was good. Ernest Hatton, operating his 150 tramcars over 59½ miles of track, now controlled a workforce totalling 965, which included 234 regular drivers, 234 conductors, 40 pointsboys, 50 depot day staff, 147 depot night staff, 15 overhead linesmen, and 50 permanent way employees. Capital expenditure on the tramways so far had amounted to £620,029, the operating costs were 69% of the total revenue, and, after allowing for interest, sinking funds, and the reserve and renewals fund, the Tramways Department had been able to contribute £12,000 to the relief of the rates. Whilst aiming to consolidate and improve what had been achieved so far, Hatton planned further expansion of the system and had persuaded the Tramways Committee to consider the purchase of additional vehicles.

Eccles Town Council had accepted a tender from Messrs. Tate & Gordon, of Cheetham Hill Road, Manchester, for the construction of the new bridge over the Bridgewater Canal. Consequently, Salford's permanent way staff commenced work in February 1904 on the tracks beyond Monton Old Bridge leading to Winton and Worsley, and new lines were also being laid in Great Cheetham Street East and Leicester Road, where a section of new highway had been cut through a portion of Broughton Park to connect Bury New Road with Bury Old Road at Half Way House. At this point, the Salford cars would gain access to the Middleton Road tramway, leased to·Salford by Prestwich, and meet Manchester cars from the Cheetham Hill Road route, which were already running by arrangement along Bury Old Road as far as the Grand Lodge entrance to Heaton Park.

The Farnworth Tramways

A press report in February 1904 seemed to indicate that Salford's tramway empire was about to extend yet further, when it was announced that an agreement had been drawn up for Salford to take over the tramways of Farnworth Urban District Council. Farnworth, a district lying between Bolton and Kearsley on the main Manchester-Bolton road, had seen itself as an important link in the tramway network which was being planned in the area, and had chosen to operate its own independent tramway in the expectation of gaining a share in profitable through routes. However, the delay of the South Lancashire Tramways Company in constructing their connecting lines to Farnworth, and difficulties in the relationship with Bolton, which town would not entertain the idea of through-running, had led to an operating loss. Farnworth owned 13 tramcars and operated on two main routes, one of which ran from Moses Gate, at the Bolton boundary, through Kearsley to Clifton, on the boundary with Pendlebury. It was hoped that Salford would agree to a connection from Station Road, Pendlebury to the Clifton terminus, a distance only of some 230 yards, and negotiations began with a view to Salford taking over operation.

Once again, press speculation proved premature. The Salford Tramways Committee considered their own Manager's views, and, in addition, commissioned the Liverpool General Manager, C.R.Bellamy, to compile a detailed report. The conclusion reached was that the Farnworth tramways were not a viable unit, and would not add to Salford's profits. It was thought that operating difficulties, such as the time early morning cars would have to leave the Salford depot, would cause too many problems. The Committee agreed that, if Farnworth had to join with anybody, it should be the South Lancashire Tramways Company. The Farnworth Council, undeterred, made a renewed offer, which was once again turned down, as Salford was not prepared to pay the rental requested. Eventually, the South Lancashire Company assumed responsibility for the Farnworth tramways in 1906.

Farnworth Council owned 13 bogie cars supplied by the G.F.Milne Company. Efforts to interest Salford in the operation of the Farnworth tramways failed, and in 1906 the cars passed into the ownership of the South Lancashire Tramways Company. Farnworth car number 3 is seen on the Clifton route.

Plans For New Cars 1904

The General Manager reported that the 150 cars in stock were barely sufficient to meet traffic requirements, and that he would need at least 20 more to work the proposed routes beyond Monton, and along Leicester Road, Bury Old Road, and Middleton Road. In June 1904 a sub-committee visited the Dick Kerr works at Preston and saw a car being built for Leicester which had an 'improved stair.' The 'improvement' was a turn of 180 degrees in the reversed spiral stair, as against the 90 degree turn on the existing cars. The visitors were impressed by this, and other features, on the Leicester vehicle, and subsequently debated whether to order cars of this type with Westinghouse electrical equipment and Brill trucks. If ordered they would have been the first cars for Salford to be built complete with top-cover.

The Tramways Committee considered ordering 20 cars similar to the Leicester model, but it was thought that the low railway bridges on some routes would prevent the use of top-covered cars. Instead, Ernest Hatton prepared a design for a single-deck combination bogie car, with seating capacity for 48 passengers, and it was agreed to commission one sample car of this sort, with others to follow if it was found to be successful in use. The final decision on the numbers and types of cars to be ordered was deferred until the sample single-deck car had been tested in service, but an order was placed for two multi-purpose permanent way vehicles, described as 'rail cleaning and water cars,' at a cost of £1,082 each. Later this order was reduced to one 'watering and snow-sweeping car,' claimed to be the first of its type in the country, on the grounds that it would be better to test a car with so many purposes before purchasing a second example. A motor tower wagon, for overhead line work, which had been on loan for three weeks from Blackwell's of London, evidently did not impress, and the offer to buy was declined.

Car 78 leaving 'The Cliff' terminus on Lower Broughton Road approaches the St.Boniface's junction on its way to Weaste via Deansgate, Manchester. The car is about to move straight ahead across the junction. The single curve in front of the tram leading into Frederick Road to the left was little used, and was intended for racecourse cars returning to the depot. It was at this point that the one-way system instituted on race days began. Cars from Victoria Bridge turned left into Frederick Road to make the circuit of Castle Irwell before returning via Lower Broughton Road on the track being followed by car 78.

At this time, the Tramways Committee learned that Manchester was experimenting with a top-covered car on its Levenshulme route. It was said to be not dissimilar to Salford's Magrini covers, but its roof provided shelter for all top-deck passengers. A comparison with the Salford covers made the point that on the Manchester sample all the windows could be raised or lowered independently by the passengers. A criticism of the Salford method of allowing only the conductor to operate the window mechanism, alleged that the winding-key was often left at the depot, and that once a car was out in service, nobody could adjust the windows.

Track Extensions 1904-05

In Whitefield, Salford had reconstructed the tracks from the railway station as far as the Bury boundary at Unsworth, but, by agreement, that section was worked by Bury Corporation only. The Bury, Rochdale & Oldham Steam Tramways Company cars to Whitefield had ceased in May 1904, electric cars of the municipal undertaking replacing them as far as the boundary at Unsworth in July, and being able to proceed as far as the Salford terminus at Whitefield Station by the end of September 1904. Here, through passengers for Bury had to change from the Salford to the Bury cars, but the press confidently announced that through-running arrangements were imminent. By January 1905, Salford had also completed tracks in Whitefield in Radcliffe New Road as far as the boundary of the Radcliffe Urban District Council at the 'Goat's Gate' Hotel, but this, too, was worked by Bury cars, as Bury had negotiated the lease of the Radcliffe tramways, and Salford cars did not go there.

Salford's own new lines in Great Cheetham Street and Leicester Road opened for traffic on the 23rd October 1904, giving access to Bury Old Road and the western side of Heaton Park. From the 9th December Salford trams

were able to pass across into Middleton Road and skirt the eastern edge of Heaton Park on their way to Rhodes, at the boundary with Middleton. On the other side, services were extended beyond the Grand Lodge entrance as far as Heaton Park railway station on the 16th December, the full route commencing from Trafford Bridge, and passing via Cross Lane, Chapel Street, Deansgate, Blackfriars Street, Great Clowes Street, and Great Cheetham Street to Leicester Road and Bury Old Road. The cars were able to go further still, as far as St.Margaret's, on the 24th January 1905. Prestwich Council urged speedy connection from this point to link with the Bury New Road tracks at Besses O'Th'Barn, and a through service was promised as soon as the overhead wiring could be erected.

A change of route which had not been appreciated drew forth complaints from residents of Swinton and Pendlebury once again. The completion of the Station Road link had enabled cars for Pendlebury to return via Swinton, and vice versa, but the shortage of cars prompted a reduction in the service from a 7½ to a 10-minute frequency, and all the cars began to reverse at Swinton. Pendlebury passengers on a Swinton-bound car thus had to change vehicles to complete the journey. Protests were long and loud, and led to the former practice being restored within three months.

In Eccles, the permanent way staff completed the laying of tracks in Parrin Lane, New Lane, and Worsley Road, but the commencement of services awaited the completion of the canal bridge at Monton. In Worsley Road, the Salford tracks extended as far as the Eccles/Worsley boundary at Alder Forest, at which point it was expected to link with lines under construction by the South Lancashire Tramways Company from Atherton, through Worsley, where some necessary road-widening on the Leigh road had delayed progress.

Within the old borough boundaries, the short length of interlaced track on Oldfield Road near its junction with Chapel Street had caused some problems. The General Manager wished to relay it, but the work was deferred.

The total length of lines operated by Salford tramway services in March 1905 had increased to over 70 miles, but firm orders for the additional 20 cars had still not been placed.

The Single-Deck Combination Car, No.151.

The body of the sample single-deck car was delivered to Frederick Road Depot on the 16th March 1905. After being united with its trucks, a number of trial runs were made towards the end of the month, with a special demonstration run for members of the Council and invited guests on Friday

The 100 single-truck cars delivered in 1901-02 were fitted with new double indicator boxes in 1903-04. Cars 26 and 2, so equipped, are seen on Bury New Road at the site of the old Kersal Toll Bar, the original Higher Broughton terminus. Car 26 is outward-bound for Whitefield, whilst car 2 is returning towards Deansgate on the journey to Peel Green. This spot also boasted a cabmen's shelter, seen behind the lamp at the entrance to Moor Lane on the left.

The sample single-deck car number 151 built by the United Electric Car Company to Ernest Hatton's specification was delivered for trials in March 1905. Subsequently, another nine were ordered, but their long wheelbase caused problems on some curves, where they had a tendency to derail. On occasions they fouled the overhead standards, some of which had to be re-sited to allow adequate clearance at junctions.

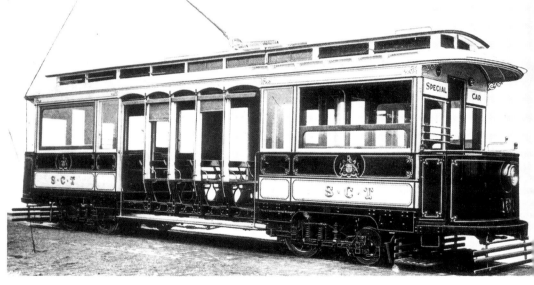

The interior view of the sample single-deck car shows the centre gangway and one of the end smoking compartments beyond the sliding door. Pull-down blinds were supposed to protect passengers in the centre portion from the elements, but to allow access, these were useful only on the off-side.

Continued from page 67

the 31st March.

The trade press described the car thus :

"The Electric Railway & Tramway Carriage Works of Preston have just supplied to the order of Salford Corporation Tramways a new type of combination car, which possesses some interesting features. The total length over the body is 31 feet 6 inches, with a platform at each end for the motorman 2 feet 9 inches long. The car is so arranged that it allows for an open compartment in the centre, for the use of smokers, and also a closed compartment at each end for non-smokers. All compartments are fitted with teak lath-and-space garden-type seats, with reversible backs, with a gangway down the centre of the car. Each closed compartment has a seating capacity of 12 and the open compartment of 24, making a total of 48. The interior of the closed compartment is handsomely finished in teak and oak. Doors are arranged at each end, the one leading into the open compartment being of the sliding type, while the one leading on to the platform is allowed to swing. Over each door is arranged an ornamental headpiece, handsomely designed, with embossed mouldings, etc. The ventilation has received special attention. In addition to having the usual line of pivoted ventilators

Chapel Street, Salford

JV 49780

A view of Chapel Street taken from the corner of Oldfield Road, looking towards Manchester, includes car number 4 heading for Heaton Park via Middleton Road, on which route it will pass over the new tracks in Great Cheetham Street and Leicester Road. Car 90 with Magrini top-cover, is on the Pendlebury route. Note the 'ALL CARS STOP HERE' sign on the centre pole. It was near this spot that Henry Collins, inventor of an automatic point-changer, had his tailor's shop.

on each side of the clerestory roof, the large windows are arranged to drop. An efficient raising and lowering device is provided, which enables the windows to be opened to any desired position from the driver's platform. Parcel racks are provided on each side, with brass brackets of ornamental design. The finish of the open compartment is similar to that of the closed compartments, but between the pillars are arranged waterproof spring-roller blinds, which can be drawn down to the floor, making practically a waterproof compartment. The ceiling of each compartment is of millboard, with 'Lincrusta' borders, handsomely picked-out in colours and harmonising with the general finish of the car as a whole. The underframe of the car is built up of steel channels and oak members, and is carried on two Brill maximum-traction trucks. Steps are arranged, running the full length of the open compartment on either side, from which access is gained to both closed and open compartments. Serviceable grab handles are provided on each pillar on either side of the car. All the necessary platform equipment is supplied, including the standard Salford life-guards. The exterior of the car is tastefully decorated, picked out in colours and lined. On the centre of each compartment are placed the borough coat-of-arms and other decorations in accordance with the Salford practice."

It will be noticed that Salford passengers still were not trusted to open their own windows.

The demonstration run was a lengthy one, the guests travelling from Victoria Bridge along The Crescent, Cross Lane, Regent Road, Deansgate, and Bury New Road to Prestwich and Whitefield, returning via Bury Old Road (the length between St.Margaret's and Whitefield being then complete) and Great Cheetham Street to lunch at the Town Hall. The car was driven by Clement Stancey, Depot Superintendent. After lunch, Alderman Linsley invited opinions. He told the guests that it was likely that twenty vehicles of this type would be ordered, and he regretted the delay in obtaining the sample car. His Committee were aware that the new car was longer than the existing cars, and that the lifeguard apparatus had come into contact with the tramway poles in one or two places, but that this was a matter which could be easily remedied. Councillor Pennington, from Manchester, complimented the Salford Committee on the number of experiments they had made, and said how greatly he had been impressed by the car. Amongst the general admirers, one of whom claimed the car gave the advantage of open travel but with dry seats, a lone detractor was a councillor who said he hoped there would be no more cars of this type. He thought it would be cold in the winter, would cost nearly as much as a double-deck bogie car, but could carry fewer people. He was concerned about the danger to passengers who might lean out of the open sides and be hit by poles. But he was in a minority - others drew attention to American practice, and said how popular single-deck combination cars were proving elsewhere.

The demonstration run of the car he had designed took place on the final day of Ernest Hatton's reign as General Manager, and tributes were paid to him at the conclusion of the lunch.

The Departure of Ernest Hatton

In December 1904 the City Council of Newcastle-Upon-Tyne had debated the terms upon which they would invite applications from persons wishing to succeed Mr.Le Rossignol as General Manager of their electric tramways. Although their car mileage at that date was not to be compared with Liverpool, Manchester or Leeds, the councillors resolved, as one of them put it, to "pay the price to get a good article." Consequently, the post was advertised at £700 per annum with increases of £50 for two years, which was a relatively high salary for that period. The vacancy attracted 83 applicants, amongst whom were the General Managers from Ayr; Blackpool; Birkenhead; Bournemouth; Brighton; Burnley; Burton-on-Trent; Cork; Dundee; Erith; Ilford; Lowestoft; Middlesbrough; Nelson; Newport; North Staffordshire; Oldham, Ashton & Hyde; Oxford; Paisley; Plymouth; Preston; Southend; South Lancashire Tramways; Stalybridge, Hyde, Mossley & Dukinfield; Sunderland; Taunton; Tyneside; West Ham; and Wolverhampton, plus many deputies and chief assistants. One of the other applicants was C.H.Chester, the Salford Traffic Superintendent, who found himself in competition with his own General Manager, Ernest Hatton.

The members of the appointing committee in Newcastle were nothing if not thorough. After considering all the applications, six persons were selected for interview. As a result, the short-list was reduced to two, namely Ernest Hatton from Salford, and H.E.Yerbury, Chief Engineer and Deputy Manager of Sheffield Corporation Tramways. A sub-committee, including the Mayor of Newcastle, had then visited both Salford and Sheffield to make further enquiries about the candidates. On the 23rd February 1905 the Mayor reported to the full Council the details of a meeting he had had with the Mayor of Salford and the Chairman of the Salford Tramways Committee: *"They spoke in the very highest terms with respect to Mr. Hatton. They said they would be extremely sorry if there was any likelihood of losing him; and that if the Tramways Committee had their own way, he would not be allowed to leave Salford under any circumstances whatever. ..... The authorities of Salford spoke of Mr.Hatton in every way as a gentleman whose services we might be proud to obtain."*

The two candidates were then interviewed by the full Council, and on a vote, Mr.Hatton was declared to have been duly appointed, and subsequently arranged to take up his post as from the 1st April 1905.

In Salford, Ernest Hatton's chief assistant, George William Holford, then aged 34, who had commenced his career with Salford Corporation almost twenty years earlier, first as a clerk in the Borough Treasurer's Department, then in the Town Clerk's office, before joining the Tramways Department, was declared General Manager-designate at a salary of £300 per annum, rising by £50 per year to £500. Though he did not possess the electrical engineering qualifications of Ernest Hatton, there was some pride in the fact that he had been "reared in the menagerie," as one councillor put it. Holford's expertise in commercial management was to be balanced by a re-arrangement of senior posts on the engineering side.

Orders For New Cars Decided

The new General Manager placed Ernest Hatton's single-deck car into service on the long Peel Green to Whitefield route. In mid-April the members of the Tramways Committee met to consider their order for new vehicles. The euphoria surrounding the trial run of the new car seemed to have evaporated - only two members wanted 20 single-deckers of that type, seven voted to have 10, whilst three recommended only 5. Subsequently, the contract awarded to the Preston firm (by then called the United Electric Car Company) was split - 9 more single-deckers were ordered, together with 10 double-deck single-truck covered cars, as seen on the visit to the works. Various modifications were stipulated - the single-deck cars were to have fixed sashes, instead of the drop windows as on the sample car, thus saving £12 per car. The top-covers on the double-deck cars were to be of the short-canopy type, as it was felt that a full-length canopy would place extra weight on the ends of the cars and increase the likelihood of rocking.

In the meantime, G.W.Holford, with only 151 cars, managed to commence services on the St.Margaret's to Besses O'Th'Barn length of Bury Old Road on the 17th April, thus connecting with the existing Bury New Road route into Whitefield. In Eccles, services over the new canal bridge began on the 1st June 1905, offering a second route to Peel Green via Parrin Lane, Winton and New Lane. The length of line between Winton and the Eccles boundary at Alder Forest lay complete, but unused. The South Lancashire Tramways Company had not yet finished the linking line from Worsley, but the local press, optimistic as ever, proudly announced that it was now possible to travel from Liverpool to Manchester by electric car - "except for a small section of about two miles between Boothstown and Winton."

The Bye-Laws And Regulations

In 1904 the Salford Corporation drew up a new set of bye-laws to govern the working of the tramways, and also published the Board of Trade regulations concerning the vehicles, the compulsory stopping places, and their speed. In respect of the latter, it may be noted that the maximum speed allowed was twelve miles per hour (increased to 16 in the 1925 version) on clear and straight lengths of track as listed in detail in the regulations. Other specified sections of track were limited to ten, six, or four miles per hour, that portion of the regulations ending: *"At all other places"* (i.e. any not mentioned by name) *"the speed shall not exceed the rate of eight miles per hour."* The tramcars were not equipped with any instrument for measuring the speed of travel, and the rate of progress was thus solely at the estimate of the driver.

The Bye-Laws were principally concerned with the behaviour of passengers on the tramcars, listing what they were NOT permitted to do, and what the actions of the driver or conductor should be in any case of a breach of the rule. Item 17, for example, read: *"No person afflicted with any infectious or contagious disease shall board, enter, or travel on any Car, or attempt to do so. And no Driver or Conductor shall suffer or permit any such person to do so."* Other bye-laws governed offensive language, conduct, and

Continued opposite

The new bridge necessary before the tramway could pass over the Bridgewater Canal at Monton was completed by contractors for Eccles Council in 1905, and services to Winton began in June. In this photograph, taken from the platform of Monton Green railway station, car 75 has just mounted the crest of the bridge from Parrin Lane, inward-bound for Deansgate. The off-set position of the trolley mast may be seen. Note the tram stop on the summit of the canal bridge. Below the photographer's position was a notice warning top-deck passengers to keep their seats and not to touch the overhead wires as the tram passed beneath the railway bridge. (Photo W.Boden.)

Car 10, its crew posing for the photographer at the end of Parrin Lane, Winton, displays a window notice which reads 'MONTON & WINTON via Eccles Old Road, FOR WORSLEY.' Salford's reluctance to work the portion of track between Winton and Worsley Court House led to a prolonged dispute with Eccles Council, and meant that passengers for Worsley had to walk from this point.
(Photo courtesy Salford Local History Library.)

George William Holford, a Broughton man, became General Manager of Salford Corporation Tramways in 1905. His career included spells as Secretary and President of the Municipal Tramways Association.

clothing, etc., any person found guilty of infringing any one of them being liable to a penalty not exceeding forty shillings. The first prosecution under the new bye-laws was of a person who was alleged to have disregarded rule 16 : *"No person shall enter, board or leave, or attempt to enter, board or leave any Car whilst in motion."* The Magistrate, in ordering the defendant to pay costs, was sympathetic, and admitted that he, too, had found it convenient to board a moving tramcar at times when it was going slowly, rather than have to stop the car. Perhaps, he said, he had been equally guilty with the defendant !

The Royal Visit, 1905

On the 13th July 1905 King Edward VII and Queen Alexandra visited Salford for the purpose of officially opening the large new dock which had been constructed by the Manchester Ship Canal Company on the site of the former racecourse. After performing that duty, the royal party passed along Cross Lane to Peel Park, and then to Oldfield Road, where the King unveiled the memorial to the Lancashire Fusiliers, before moving on to join the royal train at Victoria Station.

Both Manchester and Salford prepared elaborately decorated and illuminated tramcars to celebrate the occasion, and both vehicles toured their respective main routes for several days. On the day of the visit, the Salford

vehicle, one of the bogie cars supplied by the British Electric Car Company, possibly number 132, was drawn up at Windsor Bridge, on the route of the royal procession, where it was hoped it would be seen by the King and Queen.

There were numerous associated events connected with the royal visit (bands playing in the parks, and so on), and it was reported that tramway receipts reached record levels during those few days. Salford's takings amounted to £1405.

On the occasion of the visit of King Edward VII and Queen Alexandra to open a new dock on the Manchester Ship Canal on the 13th July 1905, an elaborately decorated and illuminated tramcar was stationed near Windsor Bridge on the route of the royal procession. Afterwards, it toured many routes on the system. One of the British Electric Car Company bogie cars was selected for this purpose, thought to have been number 132. It is seen here opposite the Windsor Castle Hotel, with the Salford Hippodrome centre left. The tramcar's staircases were removed temporarily. It is recorded that when the tramcar passed during darkness, the heat from the many lamps could be felt by spectators on the pavement.

...afford Park had been purchased in 1896 by a syndicate aiming to develop ...as an industrial estate. The British Gas Traction Company, then working line at Lytham, was persuaded to operate a service of gas-engined ...mcars between the Trafford Road entrance and Barton. This view of ...afford Park Post Office in 1901 shows the still-rural nature of the Park, ...which the four gas trams had little chance of making a profit during the

early years. The gas trams ran on railway-type single-track with passing loops, which they shared with goods trains. The line, passing to the right of the Post Office, leads to the Lake, Trafford Hall, and Barton, on the route of what was later to be designated Trafford Park Road, whilst the unpaved track to the left of the Post Office became Ashburton Road.

(Photo A.E.Bradburn.)

...e Trafford Park Tramways

...afford Park, originally a rural estate lying on the other side of the River ...vell to the south of Salford, between Stretford and Manchester, had been ...rchased from the De Trafford family in 1896 by the Trafford Park Estates ...mpany. Headed by Marshall Stevens, who had played a major part in the ...nstruction of the Manchester Ship Canal, the Company had seen possi-...ities in the location of the Park alongside the new terminal docks, and had ...termined to develop it as Britain's first industrial estate. Before any land ...d been occupied, Marshall Stevens, realising the importance of having a ...stem of public transport in the Park to carry workers to and from the ...ctories, had invited the British Gas Traction Company, then operating ...s-engined tramcars at Lytham, to provide a passenger service on a line ...ich was being constructed from the Trafford Road entrance on the ...stern side, to Barton at the western end of the Park. The Manchester ...rriage and Tramways Company had declined to provide a service, ...sumably because its officials, knowing the rural nature of the Park, could ... no possibility of making a profit at that time. Its horse-trams on the ...anchester to Stretford route came no nearer than the Chester Road, Old ...afford, end of Trafford Road. In the event, the Gas Traction Company ...ened a service in July 1897, using only one car, and, after an unfortunate ...rt and an interval during which no cars operated, began again in April ...98 with four cars, working from a depot near the Barton entrance to the ...rk.

... that time, most of the Park was still farmland, with deer-park, lake, and ...ractive picnic spots, but with very few potential passengers except on fine ...nmer weekends. Consequently, the Gas Traction Company revenue was ...remely low for most of the year, and rose only on occasions when special ...ents took place, such as the visits of Barnum and Bailey's Circus, troop ...views, or agricultural shows. It was not surprising that the Company went ...o liquidation in 1899, with debts which included one to Salford ...rporation for the supply of gas. The Estates Company itself was obliged ... purchase the gas tramway, and pay the outstanding bills, in order to ...intain services.

...other factor making the success of the gas tramway less likely was that ...ne of the earliest firms taking land in the Park chose sites contrary to ...pectations. The eastern end of the Park, nearest to Manchester city centre, ...s the portion which became industrialised first, whilst the Barton end ...nained rural. This was not so surprising, but what had not been forecast ...s that many of the early firms did not necessarily desire a frontage on the ...ks of the Ship Canal, and instead located themselves on land away from

the docks, but with rail connections to the Cheshire Lines Railway. The Westinghouse, one of the earliest and largest of the factories, opened to produce electrical equipment for tramways; the Trafford Power and Light Company, an associate of Glover's Cable Company also took space. G.Martin Brill, of the Brill Car Company of Philadephia visited the Park with a view to acquiring land for a British factory, and the British Electric Car Company leased a site on the opposite side of the road from the Westinghouse. All these undertakings were on sites removed from the gas tramway, and, apart from the obvious connections of these industries with electrical power, the Estates Company quickly realised the necessity of providing an efficient passenger service to convey workers closer to the factory gates.

In 1899 Marshall Stevens had first tried to persuade the Corporations of Manchester and Salford to include Trafford Park in their plans for proposed electric services. He had also attempted to interest the Westinghouse Company in operating an electric tramway, but the Westinghouse officials had decided that they were not in business for that purpose, so Stevens contacted Manchester and Salford for a second time. He suggested that a tramway should be built to form a large loop at the Trafford Road end of the Park, where the new factories were concentrated. As a stop-gap measure, W.H.Gaunt, the gas tramway manager, purchased four second-hand horse-drawn omnibuses in 1900 and began a workmen's service from Pendleton into Trafford Park. This lasted until the Salford horse-trams began to run to Trafford Bridge, after which passengers had to alight and walk the few yards across the swing bridge to the Park entrance.

Manchester and Salford, busy with their own schemes, gave apparently favourable consideration to the idea of running into Trafford Park, but had other priorities. For Salford, a major problem to be faced was the method of arranging a tramway crossing of the Trafford Road swing bridge, although in April 1902, when the Trafford Road lines were certified by the Board of Trade, it was recorded that the lines continued to the centre of the bridge, and were to be continued on the other side by Manchester ready for inspection. For both Corporations, another consideration was the fact that a few yards of roadway leading to the Park entrance actually lay within the area governed by the Stretford Council. The plans of the Stretford Council to reconstruct its horse-tramways and lease them to Manchester, were delayed by extended litigation with the Carriage Company, the owners of the original tracks, over the terms of purchase. By April 1902 Salford electric tramcars were running to one side of Trafford Bridge, and later in the year Manchester cars reached Old Trafford at the Stretford boundary, but the likelihood of speedy connection into Trafford Park seemed remote. The directors of the Estates Company concluded, somewhat reluctantly, that they must construct and operate an electric tramway of their own. Engineers were commissioned to lay the new Trafford Park Estates Company tramway, and five double-deck, open-top, single-truck tramcars were ordered from the British Electric Car Company. The gas tramcars ran on railway lines of standard gauge, and, indeed, shared the use of those lines with steam locomotives hauling wagons to and from the factories, but it was decided that the electric tramway would have exclusive use of its own normal grooved tramway rail in the centre of the roadway. The standard gauge of 4 feet 8½ inches was chosen again, and terms were provisionally agreed to connect with, and have running powers over, the Manchester and Salford tramways as soon as possible. A tram shed, for the electric cars only, was erected in a corner of the British Electric Car Company's site, for that Company had agreed to maintain and repair the cars in return for the right to hold exhibition runs of their new vehicles along the Trafford Park tracks. The Salford General Manager, Ernest Hatton, liaised with W.H.Gaunt, and the pair drew up plans for joint running as far as the Barton end of the Park, but, sadly, these plans came to nothing because of the delay in gaining Council approval for the construction of the junction in the Stretford portion of Trafford Road. Less ambitious, curtailed arrangements perforce catered for the electric cars to run only around a loop some 2.5 miles long, commencing in Trafford Park Road and passing via Ashburton Road and Third Avenue to join Westinghouse Road before returning to the entrance near Trafford Bridge.

Whilst awaiting the completion of work on the track and overhead wiring, W.H.Gaunt had engaged traffic staff, and, with Ernest Hatton's co-operation, the new crews began training on Salford routes.

Ill-feeling between the Estates Company and the Stretford Urban District Council was evidenced when the Company won its case against the Council at a Board of Trade hearing in March 1903. The Council had sought to impose restrictions on the Trafford Park tramway, but it was confirmed that the roads within the Park were not public highways, and that the Company would be allowed to decide as it thought fit. The Council was informed that the time to impose restrictions would come only if they gained Parliamentary powers to take over the roads on the estate. This rebuff no doubt contributed to the Council's reluctance to approve the plans for a junction to connect the Park tramways with those of Manchester and Salford at Trafford Road entrance.

The Trafford Park Electric Tramcars

The five new electric cars for Trafford Park were ready in the British Electric Car Company Works in June 1903. A smart blue livery had been chosen, and the cars were numbered 5 to 9 inclusive, as the gas cars retained numbers 1 to 4. The new service began on the 14th July 1903, from which date the four gas cars, in their 'dirty green' livery, worked a shortened route meeting the electric tramway at the Post Office, near Third Avenue, running from that point through the still-rural part of the Park to Barton. The electric tramcars displayed the destination 'BARTON,' on their departure from the Trafford Road end of the Park, perhaps a reflection of Gaunt's earlier plans. But they did not, in fact, run that far. Passengers wishing to make the full journey had to change to a gas tram at the Post Office, when the destination blind of the electric cars would be altered to read 'TRAFFORD.' as they began the return portion of the 'Westinghouse Circle,' as it was named on the tickets.

W.H.Gaunt had recommended an order for six single-truck cars at a price of £532 each, but on visiting the British Electric Car Company works in April 1903 he had been surprised to find a bogie car under construction for the Trafford Park tramway. The explanation was that the Car Company had offered to supply the Estates Company with one bogie car, identical with the type recently ordered by Salford, at the same price as a single-truck car, on condition that it could be used for demonstration purposes. It was evident that Marshall Stevens had omitted to inform W.H.Gaunt of this arrangement. The larger car was delivered a few weeks after services commenced. Although identical with the bogie cars then being supplied to Salford, it was officially listed as seating 75, 45 on the upper deck, but only 30 on the two longitudonal seats in the lower saloon, two fewer than the Salford figure. With an allowance of 15 persons per side on the lower deck

With the opening of the Trafford Park electric tramway in 1903, the gas car route was shortened, but not abandoned. Car number 7 displays the destination 'BARTON,' but passengers wishing to travel to Barton would change at this point to a gas tram, starting from the other side of the Post Office building, whilst the electric car would return around 'Westinghouse Loop' to the Trafford Road entrance. In contrast to the earlier illustration, it may be noted that by 1903 Ashburton Road had been properly surfaced.

perhaps it was assumed that Trafford Park workmen were stouter than the average Salford passenger. Another difference was that whereas the Salford cars were equipped with four 25-horse-power motors, the Trafford Park bogie car had only two, rated at 35-horse-power, which were perhaps considered sufficient for the 2½-mile route. Oddly, this car, which became number 10 in the Trafford Park fleet, was painted in the Salford livery of maroon and cream from the moment it joined its blue companions. Also from the outset, in contrast to the other electric cars, it was equipped with a double-line indicator box, as on the Salford cars, which appeared to be an extravagance in view of the fact that only the top portion was used, and even that for only two destinations, 'BARTON' and 'TRAFFORD RD.'

Gaunt was faced with the problem of transporting thousands of workpeople to and from the factories during two short periods of the day, and decided that the solution lay in the use of trailer cars. He had purchased three ex-Bristol horse-trams for this purpose, to be towed in morning and evening peak periods by the electric cars. He also ordered a new trailer car at a cost of £154 from the B.E.C.Company. This vehicle was rather like a railway coach, and was fitted with self-registering turnstiles, supplied by the Salford firm of Sir W.H.Bailey, Sir William Bailey being a director of the Trafford Park Estates Company. The turnstiles were intended to assist the conductor in collecting fares on entry to the car, for the short two-or-three minute journey did not allow very much time for the crew to move around and issue tickets. The new trailer could accommodate 100 passengers, and was regularly towed by the bogie car on the 8.23 a.m. departure from Trafford Road, when it was usually packed with workers who started at the factories at 8.30 a.m.

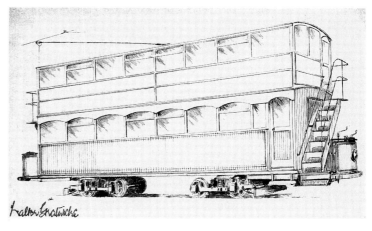

Trafford Park car number 11 was a railway-type coach, built in 1903, and used in the 'rush-hour' as a trailer towed by the electric cars. In 1904 it was adapted as a motorised car by the British Electric Car Company, and was fitted with a top-deck, which could be reached only by outside staircases from the extended platforms. As far as is known, no photograph exists of this unique vehicle, which, with seats for 132, was the largest-capacity tramcar ever to operate on a British tramway. Because of its unwieldy nature on the longer Salford routes, and as it needed two conductors, its body was destroyed in 1907. This drawing by the late Walter Gratwicke was based upon plans submitted to the Board of Trade.

After some experience of working the electric tramway, W.H.Gaunt recommended a trial with a Magrini-type top-cover, similar to a sample he had seen on a Bolton car. Milnes Voss agreed to supply one through the B.E.C.Company for £47, and this was fitted to car number 8. It differed from the Salford covers in that its roof extended over the full length of the top-deck, affording some protection to the balconies and staircases. Originally, it appears to have been unglazed at the sides.

Gaunt had ideas for altering the new trailer car, too. It had proved somewhat unwieldy in use, and had created difficulties in shunting at the Trafford Road terminus, where its towing car wasted precious minutes of the short journey time in changing ends. Gaunt therefore suggested in February 1904 that it should be adapted as a motorised car, with second-hand Brill maximum traction trucks and Westinghouse equipment, and that end platforms and a covered top-deck should be added. He stated that the structure of the trailer car was strong enough to carry a top load, as he had had the idea of a possible conversion in mind when placing the order, and thought that when altered it would be able to accommodate 190 or 200 persons. This proved to be too high an estimate, but when adapted by the B.E.C.Company, and fitted with transverse seating, it could carry 66 on each deck, total 132, plus standing passengers, making it the largest capacity car ever to be used on a British tramway. This strange vehicle entered service in its new form in May 1904, being numbered 11 in the Trafford Park fleet. The original trailer had been 28 feet 6 inches long, but the added platforms made the new total length 37 feet 6 inches, and it was over 16 feet 7 inches high. The turnstiles were removed, being replaced by swinging doors, and because of its large capacity on the short 'Westinghouse Circle' and because the top deck could be reached only by separate outside staircases, this large car always needed two conductors to collect fares in the few minutes available.

Plans To Connect Trafford Park To The Manchester And Salford Tramways

By the time the large workmen's car entered service, negotiations had re-opened with a view to either Manchester or Salford taking over the Trafford Park Tramways, and a scheme was revived for equipping the line for electric cars as far as Barton. An agreement was drawn up in May 1904 making arrangements for vehicles of the two Corporations to run into the Park, and the Estates Company indicated its willingness to dispose of its tramcars if the services were to be run by the two larger undertakings. On behalf of the Stretford Urban District Council, Manchester Corporation promised to complete forthwith the connecting junction at the Trafford

Trafford Park electric car number 6 stands at the Trafford Road entrance in July 1905 ready to make its circuit of the 2.55 miles of the 'Westinghouse Loop,' during which it would pass over 34 railway crossings, for by that date rail connections had been laid to most of the large factories. A blue livery, lined-out in gold, was adopted for the Trafford Park electric cars, and, unlike Manchester and Salford, advertising was allowed on the upper deck panels. The fleet numbers of the electric cars began at 5, as the gas cars were numbered 1 to 4.

Road entrance to the Park, but by January 1905 it had not done so. The Estates Company grew impatient, and threatened to commence an action against Manchester and Salford Corporations claiming £10,000 damages for breach of agreement in failing to fulfil their obligations to run tramcars in Trafford Park by the date agreed. The Company also began to prepare a Parliamentary Bill which sought powers to run their own trams into Manchester.

The Estates Company agreed to withdraw its action on the understanding that the two Corporations would institute services at the earliest possible moment. The connecting junction was installed by the end of February 1905, but services from Salford could not reach the Park until the Trafford Road Swing Bridge had been adapted and electrically equipped, which work was to be undertaken by the Manchester Ship Canal Company's Engineer. The Estates Company accepted that Salford tramcars could not run into the Park as yet, but saw no reason why Manchester should not commence a service. Indeed, there were at least two occasions when special cars from Manchester made unauthorised journeys beyond the Trafford Road entrance, because of inadvertent mistakes by their drivers when conveying parties of visitors to a factory. These instances were noted by Trafford Park tramwaymen and duly reported to Marshall Stevens, who himself requested permission for one of his own cars to make a special run in April 1905 with a party of Directors from Trafford Park to the Victoria Hotel in Manchester. He assured J.M.McElroy that : "*The car shall be driven and conducted by men who have been passed by your Department as being proficient both in driving and conducting, under the directions of our Mr.Gaunt, who will accompany it.*" It is not known whether this permission was granted. The Manchester General Manager was more likely to have offered the hire of one of his own cars.

The Trafford Road Swing Bridge

The Manchester Ship Canal Engineer had to overcome the problem of the gaps in the tramway at each side of the swing bridge, and also to ensure that both track and overhead wires aligned accurately whenever the bridge swung back into position. The difficulties were resolved, but there remained anxiety over the possible dangers. To allay fears, railway-type signals were erected 150 yards away on each side of the bridge. These

moved to the 'DANGER' position when the bridge was opened to allow ships to pass along the canal. As a further safeguard, in case the signal should not be seen, or be disregarded by the motorman, 'catch points' were set into the track on the approach to the bridge. The points were worked electrically by the bridgemaster at the same time as he set the signals to 'DANGER' and opened the bridge. The local newspaper reported that "*The closing of the points will mean that the car is carried off the usual track, so that the danger of a vehicle crashing into the gates which are thrown across the roadway when the bridge is open will be almost entirely removed.*" There is no recorded instance of this ever happening. The arrangements were inspected on the 13th October 1905, and approved subject to cars stopping at the signal before reaching the canal bridge.

The Trafford Park Agreement

It may be that some private arrangement had been reached between Manchester and Salford that neither would begin services until the other could do likewise, but the threatened lawsuit was still pending in mid October 1905. Whatever the reason for the delay, through services into Trafford Park from both undertakings were planned to commence when Salford cars could cross the swing bridge, and the date set was Monday, the 30th October 1905. From this date, Manchester took a 21-year lease of the Trafford Park electric tramway, and granted running powers to Salford. Each Corporation ran a 15-minute service from Manchester's Deansgate to

Preparations for linking the Salford lines to the Trafford Park system were delayed by the problem of aligning track and wires at the Trafford Road Swing Bridge. In this view, track has been laid, and the overhead wires tied back ready for connection. A workman appears to be cleaning out the points at the crossover. Salford tramcars may be seen at their Trafford Road terminus on the far side of the bridge. Until the junction was successfully effected, workers from the Salford side had to cross the bridge on foot to join the Trafford Park tramway, whose cars started from a point a few yards behind the camera position.   (Photo Charles Wilkinson.

Trafford Park, Manchester cars travelling via Old Trafford and Chester Road whilst the Salford service arrived via Trafford Road and the Swing Bridge. The two services thus offered a 7½ minute frequency inside the Park, with many extra cars to and from various parts of Manchester and Salford during peak periods. Manchester also provided an additional service from the Park entrance to the city, and similar services were operated by Salford from the other side of Trafford Bridge. However, no cars were allocated to work round the Trafford Park loop alone, as the Estates Company cars had done.

Trafford Park Tramways: Time Table

Town (St. Mary's Gate)	Old Trafford Bar (for Trafford Park)	Trafford Park Entrance (for Westinghouse)	MANCHESTER Cars (Red colour)	Westing-house (for Town)
Minutes past the hour				Mins. past hour
8	8	11	Weekdays and Sundays	5
23	23	26		20
38	38	41		35
53	53	56		50
			Weekdays.	
7 8 a.m.	7 23 a.m.	7 26 a.m.	...... First Car.	7 35 a.m.
11 23 p.m.	11 38 p.m.	11 41 p.m.	...... Last Car	11 5 p.m. to Town
				11 20 11 35 & 11 50 p.m. to Princess Road Depôt only
			Sundays.	
9 38 a.m.	9 23 a.m.	9 26 a.m.	...... First Car......	9 35 a.m.
10 38 p.m.	10 53 p.m.	10 56 p.m.	...... Last Car	10 35 p.m. to Town
				10 50 and 11 5 p.m. to Princess Rd. Depôt only

Town (Deansgate)		Trafford Park Entrance (for Westinghouse)	SALFORD Cars (Chocolate colour)	Westing-house (for Town)
Minutes past the hour				Mins. past hour
10		5	Weekdays only	12
40		35		42
5 40 a.m.	....	5 35 a.m.	...... First Car......	5 42 a.m.
11 10 p.m.	....	11 35 p.m.	...... Last Car	11 12 p.m. to Town
				11 42 to Frederick Rd. Depôt

Additional Workmen's Cars will also run in the mornings and evenings.

Manchester and Salford tramcars began running regular services into Trafford Park in October 1905. Each corporation ran a 15-minute service at first, giving a 7½ minute frequency within the Park, but by the time this timetable was issued in 1911, the Salford service was half-hourly, though many extra cars were run on morning and evening workmen's services. Note that the timetable refers to the Salford cars as 'chocolate colour.' The Trafford Park electric cars were purchased by Salford, but the gas trams remained in the ownership of the Estates Company and continued to work independently on the Post Office to Barton section until 1908.

The first day of joint operation could not have been considered a success. A letter from the Westinghouse to Manchester Corporation claimed that 70% of the workforce had arrived late on that Monday due to an insufficient number of tramcars working round the Trafford Park loop during the morning peak period. Workers travelling by other services to the Trafford Road entrance, had been unable to board cars working into the Park, as these had all been full. Complaints about the inadequate service persisted for some weeks, and several factory managers requested more extra cars between 8.00 and 8.30 a.m., and at 5.30 p.m. Petitions from workers were submitted, suggesting, sensibly, that cars returning empty from the Westinghouse should reverse at Trafford Road to travel round the loop once again, thereby providing extra capacity within the Park. For some reason, the tramway managers seemed reluctant to adopt this idea.

The Trafford Park Estates Company retained its own tramway inspectors to check on workings into the Park, and they were diligent in the investigation of overcrowding and shortage of extra cars. Other workers from the Estates Company's electric tramway were absorbed into the employ of Manchester or Salford, as had been promised to W.H.Gaunt. Gaunt himself had departed to become agent for the First Garden City at Letchworth, but continued to be consulted by letter on matters relating to the tramway.

The Estates Company had agreed to dispose of their electric tramcars, but continued to operate the four gas cars on the line between the Post Office and Barton. Salford had promised to purchase the seven electric cars, but during November they remained unused in the Trafford Park car shed whilst the two parties attempted to agree a price without resort to arbitration. Pending the acceptance of the electric cars by Salford, a rather curious working took place. The Estates Company wrote to J.M.McElroy in

Manchester to say: "We shall be glad to make the week's run of our Car to Salford so as to be able to deliver the Car to Salford as soon as possible, and if convenient to you we will run it, mornings and evenings, during the week commencing on Thursday next. We propose to run the car from the Westinghouse Corner at 6.25 a.m. and 5.35 p.m., and from the Salford side of Trafford Bridge at 6.40 a.m. and 5.50 p.m." Bogie car number 10 was selected for this duty, and worked the stated journeys on Thursday and Friday, the 9th/10th November 1905, but on the Saturday, when factories closed at noon, the second duty was timed for 12.05, returning at 12.15 p.m., and on the Sunday only the morning journey was made. These seven journeys must have been in addition to the normal services provided by the Corporations, and were probably requested by McElroy to help answer the complaints about the insufficient number of extra cars on the Trafford Park loop in the morning and evening peak periods. If this was the reason, it is not clear why extra workings were not required between 8.00 and 8.30 a.m. At the Trafford Road end, the car passed over a few yards of track outside the Park to reach Trafford Bridge. A letter dated the 21st November from J.M.McElroy read : "*I shall be obliged if you will let me have particulars of the running of your car over our track to the Salford boundary with a view to ascertaining the amount which will be chargeable to your Company in respect thereof. We shall require to know the earnings on that length, number of journeys run, and detailed particulars of your working expenses.*" The Estates Company responded, listing the journeys, the timings, and the number of passengers carried, leaving Manchester to work out the earnings and the working expenses.

The price eventually agreed with Salford for the seven electric cars was £3395. The four single-truck open-top cars were purchased at £453 each, the one with the Magrini top-cover at £501, the bogie-car similar to Salford's own at £588, and the large workmen's car at £494. The total original cost of the electric cars, with extras and conversions, was shown in the Trafford Park accounts as having been £3959. They had operated as a separate unit for some two years and three months.

The former horse-cars which had been used as trailers on the electric tramway, together with the horse-drawn omnibuses from the Pendleton route, assorted surplus plant, carts, and one Serpollet steam tramcar which had been tested in Trafford Park, were sold off at an auction in the car shed on the 10th November 1905, at which time the electric cars were still housed there. It was hoped that Manchester Corporation might have been interested in purchasing the depot building, but they did not wish to house cars in the Park. The electric cars vacated the shed and moved to Salford about the end of November, though it appears to have been June in the following year before the Estates Company received the money for them.

The Trafford Park gas trams continued to operate from their own shed at the Barton end of the Park until May 1908, when they were replaced by a workmen's train.

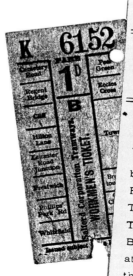

This commercial postcard bears the legend, 'Westinghouse Workers rush for cars 12 o'clock Saturday.' The location is Westinghouse Road, near the corner of Third Avenue, with the main gate to the Westinghouse Works across the railway tracks to the left. Salford bogie car 101 is bound for 'THE CLIFF,' the one behind for 'ECCLES.' Other cars would be drawn up around the corner in Third Avenue, which regularly accommodated a long line of mixed Manchester and Salford trams waiting for the factories t disgorge their workers at finishing time. An unusual feature of Traffor Park operation was that the Estates Company, having disposed of i tramcars, retained a body of tramway inspectors, with powers to boar Manchester and Salford cars to check time-keeping and ticket issue.

TABLE OF OPENING DATES OF SECTIONS OF THE ELECTRIC TRAMWAYS SYSTEM, 1901-05

Section	Opened By Electric Trams
Blackfriars Bridge to Kersal, via Great Clowes St., Great Cheetham St., and Bury New Road	4th October, 1901.
Grove Inn (Bury New Road) to Kersal	14th October, 1901.
Chapel Street to Pendleton and Irlams O'Th'Height	21st November, 1901.
Kersal (Bella Vista) via Great Clowes Street	5th January, 1902.
Oldfield Road, Regent Road, Eccles New Road (as far as Cemetery Road) ; Cross Lane, Trafford Road	4th April, 1902.
Lower Broughton Road and Sussex Street	2nd May, 1902.
Eccles New Road (Cemetery Road to Eccles Cross)	9th May, 1902.
Eccles Old Road to Peel Green, via Patricroft	3rd October, 1902.
Kersal (Bury New Road) to Prestwich Station	5th December, 1902.
Irlams O'Th'Height to Swinton Church	7th March, 1903.
Irlams O'Th'Height to Hospital Road (Bolton Road)	25th March, 1903.
Prestwich (Bury New Road) to Whitefield	3rd April, 1903.
Hospital Road (Bolton Road) to Pendlebury, and Station Road, Pendlebury, to Swinton	31st May, 1903.
Eccles Station to Monton Green	15th September, 1903.
Ordsall Lane and New Oldfield Road	9th October, 1903.
Whitefield Station to the Unsworth boundary	7th September, 1904.
Great Cheetham Street West and Leicester Road	23rd October, 1904.
Middleton Road to Rhodes	9th December, 1904.
Bury Old Road to Heaton Park Station	16th December, 1904.
Whitefield to the Radcliffe boundary	4th January, 1905.
Bury Old Road (Heaton Park Station) to St.Margaret's	24th January, 1905.
Bury Old Road (St.Margaret's) to Besses O'Th'Barn	17th April, 1905.
Monton Green to Winton, via Parrin Lane	17th April, 1905.
Winton to Peel Green, via New Lane	1st June, 1905.
Trafford Park Circle joined to Salford routes	30th October, 1905.

Consolidation and
Development of the System, 1906 - 1912.

In the Eccles area, the line from Winton towards Worsley was completed in June 1905. Salford bogie car 135 is seen on a test run in Worsley Road, Winton, by the Egerton Arms Hotel. In the following year, a little further along this road, an end-on connection was made with the South Lancashire system at the Worsley boundary. Salford Corporation showed no inclination to work this section, but granted permission for South Lancashire cars pass over the line to meet the Salford cars at Winton. Eccles Council disputed Salford's right to offer this facility, and a prolonged difference of opinion resulted in the absence of any form of service on this length of track for many years.
(Photo W.Boden.)

With the connection made to the Trafford Park lines, the Salford tramway system was substantially complete, and was able to enter upon a period of consolidation and improvement.

In 1906 the total length of tramways over which Salford services operated was as follows :-

Salford	36.5	miles.	Owned by the Corporation.
Manchester	9.5	miles.	Running powers by agreement.
Eccles	8.0	miles.	Leased.
Swinton & Pendlebury	6.75	miles.	Leased.
Prestwich	7.0	miles.	Leased.
Whitefield	4.5	miles.	Leased.
Trafford Park	2.5	miles.	Worked jointly with Manchester Corporation.

Total 74.75 miles.

Future additions and alterations to the track were destined to be only of a minor nature, and not until the mid-1920s were successful efforts initiated to extend the inter-running arrangements. At the start of 1906 the question

of the use of the South Lancashire Tramways track between Winton and Worsley, gave little indication that it was to prove a long-drawn-out dispute. In other districts, services improved as the number of tramcars in the fleet increased.

The services offered in 1906 included several changes made either in the light of experience of working the traffic, or as additional lengths of track became available for use. As agreed in the 1903 arrangement, all the routes passed along part of Manchester's Deansgate, and the April 1906 timetable listed the following services :-

ECCLES CROSS to RHODES (Middleton Road), via Oldfield Road,
    an extension of a previous route to Great Cheetham Street.
ECCLES CROSS to KERSAL BAR (Bury New Road),
    via Eccles New Road, Cross Lane, and Chapel Street.
DEANSGATE to MONTON, WINTON (for Worsley), and PEEL GREEN,
    via Eccles Old Road, returning via Liverpool Road, Patricroft, and
    Eccles.

DEANSGATE to PEEL GREEN,
> via Eccles Old Road, returning via New Lane, Winton, and Monton, the reverse of the above route.

PEEL GREEN to WHITEFIELD,
> via Eccles New Road, Regent Bridge, and Bury New Road.

PRESTWICH to PENDLEBURY,
> via Bury New Road, Great Clowes Street, Pendleton, and Irlams O'Th'Height, returning via Station Road and Swinton.

DEANSGATE to SWINTON,
> via New Bailey Street, Pendleton, and Irlams O'Th'Height, returning via Station Road and Pendlebury.

TRAFFORD PARK to ORDSALL LANE,
> via Trafford Road, Cross Lane, Chapel Street, Blackfriars Bridge, Deansgate, Liverpool Road, and Ordsall Lane, returning via New Oldfield Road and Water Street.
>
> (This route replaced the former Trafford Bridge to Deansgate service. It could not complete the full circuit because the lines connecting Ordsall Lane to Trafford Bridge had not then been constructed.)

WEASTE to WHITEFIELD,
> via Eccles New Road, Cross Lane, Great Clowes Street, Great Cheetham Street, and Bury Old Road, a new route using the Leicester Road link.

WEASTE to THE CLIFF (* Cromwell Bridge),
> via Eccles New Road, Regent Bridge, Blackfriars Street, and Lower Broughton Road. * [The change of destination title to the more specific 'CROMWELL BRIDGE' was made late in 1907, leading to protests from local residents in January 1908 who wanted the cars to display 'THE CLIFF' as formerly. 'CROMWELL BRIDGE' remained, however, but the terminus continued to be known as 'THE CLIFF,' or just 'CLIFF,' in internal literature.]

CIRCULAR ROUTES, from Trafford Bridge via Cross Lane, Frederick Road, Broughton, Blackfriars Bridge, Deansgate, Liverpool Road, and Regent Bridge, and reverse.

An impressive entrance arch, office accommodation and extensions to the car shed, were added to Frederick Road Depot in 1907, providing a more enclosed courtyard than hitherto. In this view, Seaford Road (from which there was another entrance to the sheds) is to the left, Frederick Road to the right. A preservation order has led to the retention of the arch and offices, but the sheds were demolished in 1989.

Other long journeys made unnecessarily difficult because of inability to reach reasonable agreement were those to Bury, where a change of car had to be made at Whitefield (even though tracks were connected and through running was possible), and to Middleton, where a change of vehicle was made at the short gap in the tracks at Rhodes. This page of the Salford timetable in 1906 attempted to attract through passengers.

SALFORD CORPORATION TRAMWAYS.

Manchester to Bury by Car.

THE CARS of the Bury Corporation meet those of Salford at Whitefield and a direct journey from Manchester to Bury can thus be made by Electric Car throughout.

Salford to Oldham
(BY CAR)

The Middleton Electric Traction Company's Cars running between Rhodes and Oldham meet the Salford Cars at the Rhodes terminus. A journey can thus be made by Car from Salford Docks direct to Oldham.

Time occupied	$1\frac{1}{2}$ hours.
Total distance	$13\frac{1}{2}$ miles.

Fares, $7\frac{1}{2}$d.

An interior view across the inspection pits of Frederick Road Depot in 1907 shows the Engineering Car, bogie car 131, single-deck car 153, and ex-Trafford Park car 173.

The section of track in Eccles between Winton and the Worsley boundary at Alder Forest remained unused, passengers for Worsley having to alight at Winton. The lines at the proposed junction with the South Lancashire system at Swinton Church remained unconnected, though the points were laid in on the S.L.T. side. The construction of the tramway from Farnworth through Clifton was expected to be continued by Salford, for only an extra length of some 250 yards was needed to form a junction with the existing lines at Pendlebury, and it appeared that Salford was prepared to lease that length to the South Lancashire Company. The local press commented that the long-desired connection of the tramways between Manchester and Bolton by the most direct route was about to be realised. A later report corrected this forecast. An editorial said that "*it would be hard to find a greater case of fatuity*," for the reporter had learnt that as a result of a conference between the South Lancashire Company and the Swinton & Pendlebury Council, the terms provided for a space of one yard to separate the ends of the tracks. The problem appeared to centre around demands made by the Swinton and Pendlebury Council, which neither Salford nor the S.L.T. Company was prepared to meet. The editorial expressed the hope that the setback was merely temporary lest "*the chance of a valuable link between two tramway systems and of through running is thrown away.*" But here again, as at the other end of Station Road, the tracks remained unconnected.

Similarly, the projected through-running arrangements to Bury, though physically possible via the Whitefield tracks, did not materialise, and passengers had to change cars at Whitefield Station. In April 1905 a Bury car made a brief excursion into Salford territory on a trial run from Whitefield to Heaton Park along Bury Old Road, but it was found that there was insufficient clearance for the trolley arm to pass under the low bridge at Besses O'Th'Barn. On the 19th January 1907, and on special occasions thereafter, Salford tramcars ran as specials between Whitefield and Gigg Lane, the home of Bury Football Club, the first such service being for a match between Bury and Manchester City, as Bury had insufficient cars to cope with the expected volume of traffic. But the anticipated through-running was still some 20 years in the future.

The only piece of new track constructed during the period was the extension of the Ordsall Lane lines by 260 yards of double-track to form a junction with existing lines in Trafford Road near to the Swing Bridge. This was not completed until March 1908, when the new junction enabled the Trafford Park service to complete the figure-of-eight.

Extensions to the Frederick Road Depot were planned to cater for the projected increase in the fleet and to augment its workshop facilities. The original depot had been designed to accommodate up to 180 four-wheeled cars, but with the introduction of the bogie cars and the opening of new routes, greater capacity was required. Office accommodation at the car shed was also being expanded, and it was suggested that the Central Offices should be moved from Blackfriars Street to Frederick Road. This latter proposal was rejected on the grounds of economy, efficiency, and convenience, it being argued that it was better to have the General Manager's office 'as near to the heart of the system as possible.' The extensions to the Frederick Road Depot, and the construction of the main entrance arch and offices were completed and officially opened by the Mayor on the 17th July 1907.

The summary of traffic returns for the year ending March 1906 showed that the car miles run totalled 5,257,223, and that nearly 42 million passenger-journeys had brought receipts of some £223,032. The breakdown of the value of the tickets issued, indicates that the bulk of the revenue came from the penny fares on the shortest journeys. The 5d and 6d tickets were for return journeys.

Value Of Ticket	Number Sold	Percentage of Total
1d	29,016,294	69.0
1½d	7,671,254	18.35
2d	1,980,094	4.73
2½d	1,591,717	3.81
3d	941,755	2.26
3½d	589,383	.41
5d	5,232	.01
6d	11,810	.03

The gross profit for the year was £79,713, of which £13,000 was contributed towards the relief of the rates.

Soon afterwards came the halfpenny fare for schoolchildren, although its initial reception was not encouraging. Special cars at the halfpenny rate were run during the school holidays to enable children to visit Peel and Buile Hill Parks, but the service was discontinued owing to lack of patronage. The Tramways Committee noted: "*We shall not be daunted by our failure. We feel that it is a worthy object to endeavour to get children into the fresh air and green fields away from the vitiated surroundings in which they too often live.*"

Another short-lived experiment was that of offering weekly workmen's tickets. It was reported that few people had taken advantage of the concession, and the Tramwaymen's Union had complained that the scheme led to much additional work for their members. It was decided to withdraw

The South Lancashire Tramways line from Atherton through Boothstown reached Worsley and Swinton in 1906. Car number 2, a G.F.Milnes product of 1902, is seen at Mosley Common on the way to Swinton via Worsley.

the weekly tickets, but to extend up to 8.00 a.m. the time limit for the issue of daily return tickets, by which early travellers were carried both ways at about fare-and-a-half. If successful, it was promised that the time limit would be further extended to 8.30 a.m.

Suggestions for through-running between Manchester and Salford were briefly considered, whereby Salford cars could have run to the main Manchester railway stations. An arrangement was proposed, by which conductors would be supplied with tickets from each undertaking to be issued in their respective areas, the cash balance to be adjusted to each authority at the end of each week. It was said that a similar method was functioning successfully and attracting more passengers in Oldham, but the plan foundered when negotiators failed to reach agreement.

The Worsley Route And The Dispute With Eccles, 1906 - 1913

The South Lancashire Tramways Company completed its track connection to the Salford system with a short branch of the Boothstown-Swinton line, 0.8 mile long, from Worsley Court House to the Eccles boundary at Winton (Alder Forest) on the 17th August 1906. At this point, the S.L.T. tracks met the Salford tracks in Eccles end-on. It was then announced: "*It is now possible to travel from Manchester to Liverpool with two changes of car.*" Then, again, on the 1st September 1906 came a notice which said that the Winton to Worsley lines were ready to open in a few days, "*closing the last link in the chain of tramways all the way from Manchester to Liverpool, a distance of 32 miles. Mutual running powers and through bookings are likely to be arranged between the various tramway authorities concerned, and while comparatively few passengers may travel the whole distance, the fact that a through car can be got for any portion of the route will be a great advantage to the public.*" C.R.Bellamy, the Liverpool Manager, had died in the previous year, but he would, no doubt, have been pleased to read this

notice. He had been a great advocate of mutual running powers, having no sympathy with the exclusive attitude of some authorities, and it had been one of his wishes to see a through service to Manchester. Once again, reports were premature.

Later in September 1906, the '*Tramway & Railway World*' reported that owing to a rumour of differences between Salford and South Lancashire tracks, a 'correspondent' had visited the point where the lines joined at the Eccles/Worsley boundary. He had measured the gauge, and had found a difference of one inch - the South Lancashire tracks were 4'8½", whereas the Salford tracks were 4'9½".

On Monday the 24th September, a trial trip was made over the South Lancashire Company's new lines in Worsley, and it was expected that Salford would come to an arrangement to work the additional length from Alder Forest to Worsley Court House, there to connect with cars on the S.L.T. Atherton - Swinton service. But, in fact, it was the South Lancashire Company which requested permission to run cars over the Eccles boundary to connect with the Salford cars at Winton. Eccles Council, whose lines were operated by Salford, replied to say that there was "difficulty in interpretation of the lease." The Board of Trade Inspector visited and approved the new lines on the 2nd October 1906, but they remained unused and Salford cars continued to work only to Winton. It seemed evident that the Salford authority had no great wish to extend the running of their cars to Worsley.

The next development came at Easter 1907, when Salford, without consulting Eccles Council, gave the South Lancashire Company permission to operate a service to Winton. On the Good Friday, Easter Sunday, and Easter Monday, 29th/31st March/1st April 1907, S.L.T. cars on the Atherton - Swinton service were diverted to Winton (Brown Cow) over Eccles tracks whilst their Moses Gate - Swinton cars ran on to Worsley Courthouse. Worsley was a popular destination at holiday periods, and it was hoped that this arrangement, evidently satisfactory to both operators, could be repeated at future public holiday times.

Unhappily, the arrangement was not welcomed by the Eccles Council, who proceeded to bar S.L.T. cars from their tracks, and argue that the Salford authority had no power to approve such workings. As Whitsuntide approached, Salford agreed to provide a service to Worsley Courthouse, and on Saturday, the 18th May 1907, Salford cars commenced running at 1.00 p.m. with a 10-minute frequency, and from 10.00 a.m. during the following Whit Week. The new service was with S.L.T. Company's agreement, and the Company was to receive 5d per car mile run on its track. The service was welcomed by an editorial in the 'Eccles Journal': "*Worsley promises to become an increasingly popular objective for holidaymakers this summer, and the influx is likely to be greatly increased by the latest innovation. This consists in the running of cars to the Courthouse by the Salford Corporation by way of Winton. The new service was started last Saturday and was fairly well patronised considering the inclement weather .... a through service will be provided each weekend, and from Monday to Saturday it will be every 20 minutes from Peel Green.*"

But the service provided by Salford proved to be intermittent, and critics, keeping a careful note of the operating days, were later to confront the Salford General Manager with the following statistics:-

1907:	June	- cars to Worsley every day.
	July	- 10 days only.
	August	- 11 days only
	September	- 9 days only.

The service was discontinued on the 29th September. During the year, Salford cars had operated to Worsley Courthouse on only 69 days, mainly Saturdays, Sundays, and Bank Holidays. The Salford Manager argued that the weekday receipts did not justify the service, but agreed with Mr. J.R.Salter, the S.L.T. Manager, that on fine summer weekends, the receipts were of a "phenomenal character." Mr.Salter declared himself ready to run a service to Winton if Salford did not wish to work that section, but for the present, there was no service at all.

In the following year, the South Lancashire Company, with Salford's approval, commenced a service to Winton on the 7th June 1908. Eccles Council determined to make difficulties. S.L.T. tramcars were boarded by police officers at the boundary, and names and addresses of drivers and conductors were noted. Legal action was threatened, and, once again, it was argued that Salford had no right to make such an arrangement. A court application by Eccles was first dismissed, and judgement was given in favour of the South Lancashire Company and Salford Corporation, whose proposed Parliamentary Bill would have given power to sub-lease sections of track. An Appeal Court reversed the decision in May 1910, however, and granted an injunction to prevent S.L.T. cars running in Eccles. Eccles agreed not to enforce this decision until the 25th June, on which day the

service from Winton to Worsley ceased once again. It was evident that Eccles Council did not give priority to the wishes of the travelling public, and the situation contrasted sharply with the amicable arrangements with Whitefield U.D.C., where Bury cars ran over track leased to Salford to connect with Salford services at Whitefield railway station.

Although Salford announced an intention to refer the dispute to the House of Lords, it was thought that the appeal might be prejudiced if any service was provided over the Winton-Worsley length in the meantime. The withdrawal of the trams did not please residents along the route.There were many complaints, and in November 1910 a petition signed by 924 persons was presented to the Board of Trade asking that authority to intervene and 'force' the tramway undertakings to provide a service. The Board of Trade officials felt that they were powerless, but wondered whether Eccles Corporation could require Salford to operate the route.

The appeal of Salford and the South Lancashire Tramways Company against the findings in favour of Eccles was eventually heard and dismissed in March 1912. At some date after this hearing, Salford must have decided to offer a service to Worsley, probably in time for the Whitsuntide traffic, but the event seems to have passed unrecorded by the press, whose pages were filled during this period with the reports and enquiries in the aftermath of the 'Titanic' disaster.

A regular route to Worsley eventually appeared in the Salford time-table for 1913. In 1917, a new agreement between Eccles and Salford for the latter to lease and work the tramways contained a clause forbidding Salford to 'assign or sub-let' any section wthout prior approval from Eccles.

The Middleton Tramways

The Salford service along Middleton Road to Rhodes terminated just short of the Middleton tramway system, there being a gap of a few yards between the ends of the tracks at that point. The lines in Middleton were operated

A commercial postcard strikingly illustrates the gap between the tracks at the Rhodes terminus in Middleton Road. In the foreground, Salford car 36 stands at the end of the line leased from Prestwich, whilst a few yards further on is a car of the Middleton Electric Traction Company, ready to commence the journey to Middleton town centre. Note the waiting room to the right of the picture, and the stop sign bearing the stage number 6. In the centre distance is the 'Rhodes Chimney,' noted for its great height.

by the Middleton Electric Traction Company, not the Council, but dissatisfaction was expressed at the lack of a through link at Rhodes, and in 1907 both Company and Council suggested that Salford should take over the running of the Rhodes to Middleton section. Salford agreed to extend the Rhodes route to Middleton centre, and to run a 15-minute service on trial for one year, the Company to take the profits, keep the track in order, and pay Salford's operating expenses. But the Company wanted Salford cars to go only as far as The Fountain, whereas Salford insisted on being able to run to the more central Market Place. In addition, it transpired that the Company wanted Salford to buy current from them, maintain the track, and pay a rent of £1000 per year. Although the General Manager admitted that a through service might increase the takings on the Rhodes to Manchester section, and much as he wished to run to Middleton for the convenience of the travelling public, he decided, as his predecessor had done in the case of the Farnworth tramways, that the cost of the proposed arrangements would be more than the extended service was worth, and he therefore recommended rejection of the scheme. It was to be the mid-1920s before Salford tramcars travelled to the centre of Middleton.

Additions To The Fleet

The nine additional single-deck tramcars which were commissioned after trials with the sample car, were allocated the fleet numbers 152 to 160, and on arrival appear to have been tried out on a variety of routes, particularly the Peel Green and Bury New Road services. At this time, the new General Manager, G.W.Holford, had announced his intention of using the 20 double-deck cars with the Magrini top-covers on the Pendlebury to Prestwich route, pending the arrival of the other cars on order.

The acquisition of the Trafford Park cars added seven to the number of vehicles available. Trafford Park bogie number 10, identical to the Salford cars 101-150, and already in the Salford livery, was re-numbered 161, and placed into service immediately. The other cars had to be repainted in the Salford colours. The large workmen's car (ex-Trafford Park number 11)

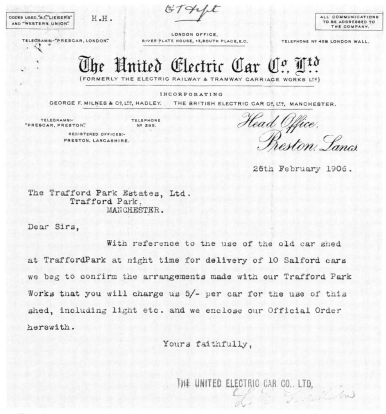

The letter from the United Electric Car Company confirming the arrangement to use the former Trafford Park tram depot for work on ten new cars for Salford. As the shed was located just across the road from the Westinghouse Works, which supplied the electrical equipment, and as from 1905 there was direct rail connection to the Salford system, it was a convenient building in which to assemble the cars before delivery.
(Trafford Park Estates Company Limited.)

took the number 162, thus keeping all the bogie cars in the same sequence, but numbers 163 to 172 were reserved for the ten cars awaited from the United Electric Car Company.

The five single-truck cars from Trafford Park were numbered 173 to 177, the car already having the Magrini top-cover (ex-Trafford Park number 8) becoming 173, presumably to follow on in sequence with the ten new covered-top cars on order. The British Electric Car Company trucks under the Trafford Park cars were replaced by Brill 21E-type in Salford.

The new cars, numbers 163 to 172, were delivered just in time to enter the stock list for the General Manager's annual report ending March 1906, when the fleet totalled 177.

The New Top-Covered Cars, 163 - 172.

The ten cars ordered from the United Electric Car Company, of Preston, were to be fitted with Brill 21E trucks, plus motors, controllers, and electrical equipment from the Westinghouse. The United Electric Car Company now incorporated the former G.F.Milnes and British Electric Car companies, and, although the Trafford Park works were unused, the new owners did not wish to dispose of the factory to a rival firm of car builders. However, the pressure on space at Preston, the tramway track connection of Trafford Park with Salford, and the proximity of the Westinghouse just across the road, made the idea of assembling the cars on the spot economically attractive. Possibly not to jeopardise any future sale of the former B.E.C. Works, in February 1906 the United Electric Car Company requested permission to use the Trafford Park Estates Company's old car shed 'at night time' for the assembly, testing, and delivery of the new cars for Salford. The reference to 'night time' probably meant only the testing of the cars on the Trafford Park tracks out of the way of normal daytime service cars, and permission was granted to use the shed at a charge of five shillings per car.

An internal memorandum, headed 'Report Of Incident,' from Mr.C.Gould, the Trafford Park Gas Car Engineer, dated Tuesday, 6th March 1906, complained that *"The United Electric Car Co. have had use of our shed since Monday, February 26th. No cars taken to Salford yet. Shed filled with United Car Co. stores. Their men using our vices and benches and mess room. Will take 6 or 7 weeks at present rate to get 10 cars through."*

Perhaps this was an indication that all was not well, for further disagreement followed, as it was considered that the U.E.C. Company had exceeded the terms of the agreement. The ten cars were duly completed and delivered to Salford, and the U.E.C. Company paid £2-10s-0d for the use of the shed. The Estates Company then submitted a further invoice, charging for the trial trips on their track, as per the former arrangement with the B.E.C. Company, and claimed also for damage to an arc lamp. The U.E.C. Company protested that they had had "nothing to do with the trial trips of these cars, not having supplied the equipments," and suggested that the account be sent to the Westinghouse. The Westinghouse repudiated liability, as, at a later date, did Salford, whose General Manager, presumably in ignorance of the previous attempts to gain payment, suggested that the Estates Company should deal with the two firms direct.

In the meantime, cars 163 to 172 had entered the Salford fleet. They were the first cars purchased by Salford to arrive complete with a top-cover, and it was noted with approval that the upper deck sides joined the floor without leaving any gaps, thus avoiding the draughts experienced with the existing Magrini covers. The General Manager placed the new cars into service on the Pendlebury to Prestwich route, on which he had used the earlier covered cars, residents of those districts thus being considered highly privileged. With the arrival of the ten new cars, G.W.Holford had 32 top-covered cars at his disposal, though the Trafford Park workmen's car did not prove very useful. The covered cars could be used only on designated routes, however. Because of low bridges carrying railway lines above the roads at Monton (Clifton Road), Besses O'Th'Barn (Bury Old Road), Great Ducie Street, and Water Street, top-covered cars could not be used on any services passing beneath those structures. None of these bridges lay within the then Salford boundary, so the authority was powerless to make any alterations to the roadway. [Years later it was discovered that an error had been made by Manchester in measuring the height of their Water Street bridge. The error was revealed when the driver of a Salford top-covered tramcar mistakenly took his vehicle under the bridge without mishap, demonstrating that the services using Water Street could have been run with covered cars from the outset.]

The top-covers on the 163-172 batch evidently did not prove strong enough to bear the swinging of the heavy trolley-boom, and substantial alterations had been made within five or six years of them entering service. Two cars, numbers 170 and 171, had their covers removed altogether, and operated

Continued on page 86

The ten new cars from the United Electric Car Company, numbers 163-172, were delivered in March 1906, complete with short-canopy roof. Car 166 is seen in Bridge Street, Manchester, leaving Deansgate for Swinton. The colour of the staircase stringer was changed to cream about this time. Note the guard collecting fares on the balcony, whilst the rear platform is in the charge of a young trolley boy. Bridge Street appears congested, as there was two-way traffic at this date, even though the tramcars operated in one direction only. The direction of tramcar traffic flow along Bridge Street and King Street West was reversed in 1930.

The top-covers of the 163-172 series cars did not prove satisfactory. Two were removed altogether, and the others were rebuilt to four-window form to give additional support to the roof. Car 167 is seen as altered. The location is Great Clowes Street, Broughton, with the Victoria Theatre on the right. In the foreground, the second track leading from Lower Broughton Road appears little used, as cars passing from Lower Broughton to Manchester reached Great Clowes Street via Sussex Street, at a junction some yards along on the left, near the third tramcar.

(Photo Charles Wilkinson.)

Continued from page 84

thereafter in open-top form. The remaining eight cars were altered so as to strengthen the upper deck sides by the provision of four sash-framed drop-windows to replace the original three.As delivered, the top-deck windows had been operated from a winder on the balcony end, as on the Magrini covers, and in appearance matched the three lower deck windows. The alterations gave an uneven look to the sides of the cars, but provided extra posts to support the roof. The opportunity was taken to incorporate a row of hinged ventilators, or 'quarter-lights,' of ruby-coloured glass above the main windows, as in the lower saloon. Two cars, numbers 164 and 165, had the original short-canopy lengthened to cover the whole balcony. It is possible that the alterations were re-builds of the original top-covers, carried out by carpenters at the Frederick Road Depot, but the new features were so major in character that they may well have been entirely new structures. In the same period, about 1911-12, similar covers appeared on at least two of the original four-wheel cars, and some of the Magrini covers were modified. Another alteration to the 163-172 cars was that the 'improved staircase' with the 180 degree turn was replaced by the more usual 90 degree pattern.

The Ex-Trafford Park Workmen's Car

The large-capacity car which became Salford 162 was not used a great deal. Its excessive length, and the fact that it needed two conductors, led the general Manager to report to his Committee in May 1907 that it was of no use to him. At the time, he was suggesting ordering 14 more top-covered cars, and disposing of the ex-Trafford Park workmen's car, so as to make a total fleet of 190. It would seem that the body of car 162 was destroyed shortly afterwards, unhappily leaving no known record of this interesting and unusual vehicle.

Orders For New Cars 1907, Fleet Numbers 177 - 200

The General Manager's proposal to purchase 14 new cars was increased to 24, and tenders were invited for their construction to a design formulated in Salford and approved by the Board of Trade in June 1907. The cars were

to have balcony-type top-covers, but would be constructed to a slightly lower height than the existing top-covered cars. They were to seat 56, 22 in the lower saloon and 34 on top. Most suppliers offered delivery within about six months, but the contracts were not approved until December. Tenders were accepted from the United Electric Car Company to supply 20 car bodies at a cost of £448-12s-6d. each, but four were ordered from Hurst Nelson at £458-17s-6d. Trucks were ordered from Mountain and Gibson, of Bury, 23 ordinary at £64-10s-0d each and 1 radial at £110-0-0. Westinghouse electrical equipment, including trolley bases, was to cost £279 per car.

Before placing this order, much discussion in the Council had centred around the 'Fair Wages' clause, for it had been alleged that the Westinghouse

The Trafford Park bogie car number 10, built by the British Electric Car Company to the same design as those supplied to Salford in 1903, was acquired in 1905, and was re-numbered 161. About 1910-11 it appeared with five windows in the lower saloon, an alteration probably intended to give additional support to the body. It remained in this form until rebuilt with enclosed top-cover and platforms in 1924-25.

Of the 24 new tramcars added to the fleet in 1908, 20 were supplied by the United Electric Car Company (numbers 177-196), and 4 (197-200) by Hurst Nelson.This maker's photograph of car 185 shows the general design, though the four Hurst Nelson cars could be distinguished end-on by the flatter appearance (i.e. less-pronounced barrelling) of the canopy above the platform. Note the patterned ruby-glass quarter lights, and the top-deck recessed bulkheads, with side-windows extending to protect part of the balcony. When some of these cars were fitted with vestibules in 1930-31, the upper-deck bulkheads and windows were retained and incorporated in the improved design.

and Hurst Nelson, in particular, underpaid their workers. An enquiry was ordered, at which both firms protested their innocence, and declared that they did pay standard rates. Hurst Nelson indignantly repudiated the criticism, and pointed out that if they had paid less than current rates, they would not have been awarded so many contracts from London. Detailed complaints about unskilled men doing craftsmen's work were answered by the Westinghouse explanation that technical advances had simplified many of the processes, and that skilled labour was not now needed for many tasks which had formerly required expert craftsmen. The enquiry found that the allegations were unproven, and the contracts were eventually confirmed. The delivery of the 24 new cars commenced about August 1908. The destruction of the large workmen's car, number 162, had left that fleet number vacant, and permitted re-numbering of car 177, an ex-Trafford Park open-top vehicle, to 162. This alteration meant that the 24 new arrivals could take the numbers 177 to 200. The United Electric Car Company bodies became 177 to 196, whilst the four Hurst Nelson products became 197 to 200. The special radial truck was placed under car 196, the others receiving the ordinary Mountain & Gibson trucks. All the new cars were equipped with the Cummins Patent Electric attachment for operating the sand boxes and brake simultaneously. On the earlier cars, some accidents had happened, particularly in wet weather, when the driver had applied the brake, but failed to depress the sand pedal. The sand pedal allowed a small quantity of dried sand to fall on to the rails close to the wheels, enabling them to exert a firm grip, rather than skid or spin. The rheostatic brake was in addition to the usual ratchet, though it was explained that the steepest gradient on the system was only 1 in 19. The ratchet brake was a rather primitive relic of the horse-tram days, by which force was applied by turning a handle to wind a chain which operated the brake shoe. Unwinding was prevented by a ratchet and pawl on the spindle. The new ratchet brakes had the 'Peacock' attachment, which worked via gearing to enable the motorman to obtain a powerful and rapid braking effect without unnecessary winding, and which, on release, allowed the chain to recover quickly. A repeat order was given to Hudson and Bowring, a Manchester firm, for the fitting of their patent lifeguards to the new vehicles, as on the other tramcars.

The 177 - 200 series cars were allocated to the Rhodes route, and afterwards became identified as 'the Rhodes cars.' The General Manager must have been gratified in September 1908 to receive a message of congratulation from residents of Rhodes complimenting the undertaking on the appearance of the new trams.

It was shortly after the delivery of these cars that the United Electric Car Company reported 'stagnation' in the electric traction industry, presumably because, most towns having by then placed and received their orders for vehicles, the boom years were over.

Rolling Stock Modifications

A plea from the motormen for better protection from the weather had led G.W.Holford to circulate other tramway managers to gain their views on

A continuous programme to improve the fleet began about 1910. Bogie car 132 was first fitted with an experimental windscreen, which was later replaced with a permanent vestibule, and in 1911-12 a balcony-type top-cover was provided, which became the pattern for the 20 covers ordered from Hurst Nelson in 1912. This photograph was taken at Frederick Road Depot in 1923, by which time the ornamental wrought-ironwork around the balconies had been replaced with a sheet metal strip.

The ex-Trafford Park car number 161, was adapted as an illuminated and decorated car to mark King George V's Coronation in 1911, and again in 1919 for the Peace Celebrations. It is seen here in Frederick Road Depot in June 1911. The staircases have been removed to allow more space for decorations. Open-top car 19 and a Magrini-roofed car are to the right.

Improvements to the fleet about 1912 included the replacement of some of the early Magrini roofs with more substantial four-window balcony-type covers, of a pattern similar to those ordered for twenty of the bogie cars. Car 89, so altered, is seen crossing the Trafford Road Swing Bridge towards the Salford side of the Manchester Ship Canal.

the provision of vestibule-ends around the platforms. Nearly all the respondents were against the fitting of vestibules - especially those who didn't have any - although the Burnley undertaking, which had never had any open-platform cars, was strongly in favour. The first result was that in 1910 a form of windscreen, open at the sides, was tested on car number 132, but after some six months a proper vestibule was constructed, and at the same time a balcony-type top-cover was fitted. Discounting the withdrawn ex-Trafford Park workmen's car, this was thus the first covered bogie car. The General Manager subsequently recommended that 20 top-covers of a similar pattern should be purchased, and a Hurst Nelson tender at £151 per car was accepted in 1912. When delivered, the covers were fitted to the British Electric Car Company bogie cars of 1903, numbers 131 to 150, but as car 132 already had its top-cover, the remaining one was allocated to car 130, the last of the Milnes bogies. No action was taken on the provision of vestibules, and the cars retained their open ends.

The ex-Trafford Park bogie car, number 161, also from the B.E.C.Company, which vehicle might have been expected to receive the extra cover, had already been rebuilt to give uneven five-window sides, possibly as a means of strengthening the body, and (with stairs temporarily removed) had been used as the illuminated and decorated car to celebrate the Coronation of King George V in June 1911. It remained in its five-window open-top form, and was used again for the 'Peace' car in 1919.

At about the same period, 1911-12, when bogie car 132 was fitted with its top-cover, there appears to have been some re-building, or replacement, of some of the early Magrini covers on the four-wheel cars. Car 88 appeared in altered form with a top-deck cover having four-windows (instead of three) and with an extended roof covering the balconies. Photographic evidence indicates that cars numbered in the fleet at that time as 44 and 61 carried similar covers from about this period. Other cars in the 81 - 100 sequence appeared to retain the original three-window covers, but were altered to have extended roofs. The covered cars are remembered as being numbered in the 80 - 100 series, and, according to the stock list, the total number of four-wheel covered cars increased by one at this time, though car 100 had its cover removed altogether and reverted to open-top state. Five of the cars (86, 94, 97, 98, 99) retained their original Magrini covers until the 1920s.

Other minor modifications to the fleet in the period before 1912, included the removal and sale of the seat carpets and the collapsible platform gates, which had rarely been used. Window curtains were retained, however, for use in summer months.

A Halley petrol-driven motor tower wagon, for overhead line work, had been purchased for £670 in 1910.

Unpopularity Of The Single-Deck Combination Cars

G.W.Holford was not an admirer of his predecessor's design of the single-deck tramcar, though he persevered in trying the ten 151-160 series cars on a variety of routes. The difficulties experienced on the trial trips with the first sample car, when its greater length had caused it to foul some of the standards supporting the overhead wires, had caused Holford to order the removal or re-siting of several poles at main junctions as early as May 1906, but the cars remained unpopular. Their tendency to de-rail at junctions was partly due to their length, but the fact that the pony wheels faced outwards pre-disposed them to this fault.

Holford indicated his willingness to dispose of the single-deckers, and in March 1907 the Blackpool & Fleetwood Tramroad Company enquired about the price required. Holford responded to say that he would accept £450 per car, considerably less than the cost when new less than two years earlier, but no further interest was shown. Later in the same year, June 1907, an offer to sell the cars to Rochdale, where General Manager J.S.D.Moffet (who was destined to become Holford's successor some 16 years hence) already operated a number of single-deck combination cars, met with a similar lack of interest. Moffet said they were not suitable for the Rochdale system, and offered to sell to Salford ten double-deck cars which he did not want.

Because of the continuing shortage of electric cars, Holford was obliged to continue to use the single-deckers. In response to numerous complaints about the dangers of the open centre-portion, where the pull-down blinds often had to be left unused to allow passengers to board and alight, and which, in any event, were found to offer little protection against the draughts and the rain, the General Manager gave orders for three of the five side-openings to be enclosed on one car only as an experiment. The car so treated was number 151, but the alteration was not made on any of the other nine, which retained their open centre.

Grievances were submitted also by the crews about their exposure to the weather on the combination cars, though this is difficult to understand, since all the motormen at that time worked on open-fronted tramcars, and conductors had to endure the open top-decks of most of the other vehicles in the fleet. Perhaps it was felt that there was a lack of shelter from side-draughts on the lower deck. Whatever the substance of their complaint, the General Manager evidently deemed it valid, and promised to withdraw the single-deck cars as far as possible during the winter months.

The adjoining district councils in whose areas Salford tramcars operated were never slow to complain. No one seemed to want the single-deck cars on their particular route. In January 1912 the cars were removed from routes in Eccles, and put to work on services to Swinton. The Swinton & Pendlebury Council immediately protested that the cars were dangerous and noisy, and that a passenger had been 'flung off' as one car turned a corner. Holford was asked to withdraw the cars, but he replied that the arrangement was merely a temporary one whilst other cars were under repair.

Within a few months of this complaint, the Equipment & Engineering Company, of Norfolk Street, London, was asked to act as an agent to find buyers for the ten cars. In June the Company notified Salford that a few enquiries had been received, and asked at what price Salford would sell. In August an advertisement, incorporating a photograph of one car which had been modified, was inserted in several issues of the trade press by the agent, mentioning that the cars were in good condition and had had 'no hard wear.' But efforts to find a buyer failed, and the General Manager eventually recommended to his Committee that the cars should be dismantled, and that new bodies should be bought in which their electrical equipment could be re-used.

Results of Municipal Operation To 1912

The year 1912 saw the completion of twelve years of municipal operation of the tramways, but only ten since the final disappearance of the horse-trams and the arrangement with Manchester had enabled the electric tramcars to operate on the longer routes. From carrying some 28 million people in 1903, the General Manager was able to report a growth to nearly 49 million passenger journeys per annum.

In the twelve months ending March 1912, the 200 cars had run a total of 5,808,369 miles, with receipts of £253,315, and average earnings per car mile of 10.46d. Highest takings were recorded in the summer months, when visits to local parks were popular, the greatest earnings coming from the Peel Green to Whitefield route, which passed by Buile Hill, Peel, Albert, and Heaton parks. Once again, the penny fares provided over 70% of the income, of which £18,000 was contributed to the relief of the rates.

The number of tramway staff had increased to a total of 1106, of whom 256 were regular drivers (with 46 spare), 256 conductors (30 spare), and 130 points boys and trolley boys. The permanent way staff numbered 57, and regular inspections of the 75 miles of track had seen a programme of renewals carried out since 1908 on those inner-city sections which saw the most intensive use. In the five years to 1912, over 13 miles of track had been re-laid with rails of the 'Sandberg' specification, which it was claimed would give longer life than the rails previously used, and all the joints had been welded by the 'Thermit' process. On another six miles of existing track, the joints had been electrically welded by the 'Tudor' process.

The 'Sandberg' process was a method developed by C.P.Sandberg of making steel with a high-silicon content, suitable for rails laid in places liable to excessive wear. It was said that rail wear was 35% to 40% less than when using ordinary steel. Welding the rail joints by the 'Thermit' process entailed using a powder in a special crucible whilst running molten steel around the butt end of the rail. The mould was designed to give a band of metal round the joint almost equal to the strength of the rail itself, and the welds offered a much smoother ride.

The route pattern in 1912 showed some slight changes from that established some six years earlier. Certain links between termini had been switched, so that the Trafford Park service went to Rhodes instead of completing the Ordsall Lane circuit, whilst the Ordsall Lane cars went to Whitefield. The Weaste to Whitefield service had been shortened to run only from Weaste to Prestwich, whereas the Cliff (Cromwell Bridge) to Weaste route had been lengthened to work as far as Eccles. Two additional routes, possibly part-day only, connected Broughton Market Place on Bury New Road with Irlams O'Th'Height and Weaste. All services continued to use a portion of Manchester's Deansgate, which always saw more Salford trams than Manchester ones.